# GOD'S
# *Questions*
# TO US

DON N. JOHNSON

Cover art courtesy of Martha Ensign Johnson: "I thought the mountains were my friends"

ISBN: 0-9916634-0-3
ISBN-13: 978-0-9916634-0-8
eBook ISBN: 0991663411
eBook ISBN-13: 978-0-9916634-1-5
Library of Congress Control Number: 2014950902
Old Stone Publishing
Santa Barbara, California

*There is only one person to whom I can dedicate this book: Martha Ensign Johnson. She is my wife and best friend. She is the artist who still teaches me to see. She is the chef who teaches me to taste. She is the mother who teaches me to love. She is the traveler who loves the new adventure. She is the restless one who teaches me to ask questions. She is the one who most lets (demands) me to be me.*

*To you, Martha!*

# TABLE OF CONTENTS

# PREFACE

*If you could ask God a question, what would it be? When I get to heaven, I want to ask God why he...?* There is this notion that we are the questioners, and God provides the answers. Since God is all knowing, all-powerful and, well, God, he has all the answers to our many, legitimate questions. Because, life is full of questions, and the older we get, the more questions arise and the deeper the questions grow. In many ways, I have more questions now in my 60's than I had in my 30's. I was much more certain then of what was true, what worked, and what should be. Now there are more ambiguities and paradoxes. My certitude about God's love and his incarnation in Jesus grows stronger, but my perplexity at the nature of the church and human behavior only increases.

On a vacation years ago in France, I read straight through the Bible over a six-week period. Every morning I arose early, made coffee, lit a candle, and curled up with the Bible and a red pen. As I began in Genesis, I noticed a question from God to Adam and Eve: *where are you?* (Genesis 3:9). Was that really a question God needed to ask? Isn't God all-seeing? Could these humans really hide from God? As I kept reading, I kept noticing more questions from God to humans: *who told you that you were naked? What have you done? Why are you angry?*

In the margin of my Bible I casually wrote "Q" in red ink beside each question and began to number them. As I kept reading the Bible, I discovered that God persistently and continually engages humans with questions. The questions did not stop in the Old Testament, but continued into the New Testament with Jesus. Jesus' questions are profoundly intriguing: *who do you say that I am? Do you want to be well? What is your name?*

By the end of that vacation, I had found over 500 questions from God or Jesus to humans…to us. Why so many questions? What do the questions mean? What does it mean that we have a God and a Savior who come to us with questions?

Now there are questions, and then there are *questions*. There are functional and mechanical questions: *where can I find the men's shoe department?* And there are rhetorical and confrontational questions: *did you just hit your sister? What kind of fool do you think I am?* And there are ritual and formal questions: *How are you? How's it going?*

Of the 500+ questions, some were functional and simple. But others operated on multiple levels beneath the surface. They could be answered in the moment, but also taken home and reflected on. The first question in the Bible of *where are you* operates on those multiple levels. We can give an address and a location, but it also elicits a reflection on our identity, role and purpose.

What intrigued me even more with all these questions was the idea that we worship a God and have a Savior who genuinely asks questions of us. What does it mean when someone asks us a question and then takes the time to intently listen and not interrupt? We have all been in those situations where a question is simply a tool to allow the questioner to expand on their opinions. That's not the way God works in the Bible. We worship a God who asks and listens for our answers.

The organization and hope of this little book is for the reader to let one question from God go with him/her for one day at a time. Let a question from God or Jesus frame and inform the day. The questions have their own power. My reflections are just my reflections. My hope is that they "prime the pump" for the reader to move the question off the page and into the heart.

I have found enormous encouragement and hope in these questions. My hope and prayer is that you do too.

# ANGELS

What do you do with angels? God makes sense and so does Jesus, but angels are not within the realm of most people's everyday experience. Angels belong to fantasy stories and mythologies. Angels are romantic imagery that grace sympathy cards and Christmas cards.

Why do I raise the question of angels? Because angels ask questions of humans three times in the Bible, and those questions need to have some context and understanding. Classically, angels are not independent spiritual operators; they only do the bidding of God. The very word "angel" comes from the Greek word "aggelos," which means "to send." Angels are always the sent-ones from God, with a message, an action, or, in this book's case, questions.

When you encounter the questions from angels later in the book, let those questions be an extension of God's questions.

# 1<sup>st</sup> ANGEL QUESTION

"DO YOU HAVE ANYONE ELSE HERE—SONS-IN-LAW,
SONS OR DAUGHTERS, OR ANYONE ELSE IN THE CITY
WHO BELONGS TO YOU?"

*GEN. 19:12*

*Who belongs to you?* That was the question the two men (angels) asked Lot. Lot lived in a morally compromised society just barely treading water. He knew that living in Sodom was dangerous, albeit profitable, business. Lot avoided trading away his soul, but just barely.

The society and culture we live in is compromised, not unlike Sodom. We work hard to stay morally balanced. But who belongs to us that might be in trouble? Who belongs to us, who is not doing as well as we think we are? The question of *who belongs to us* can be discovered by identifying the answer to who listens to us. Who pays attention to what we say and do? Can you list those persons for whom you are spiritually accountable, those who belong to you?

# PART I:
# QUESTIONS FROM GOD

## "WHERE ARE YOU?"

### GEN. 3:9

Are you kidding? Where am I? I'm right here in _____, where I've been for the last years. But location is a curious question we all like to ask. When I'm on a telephone call to a call center, I am always curious about where the person I'm talking to is located. But, *where are you* is about more than location in space. Where are you in your career? Beginning, in the middle, succeeding, or struggling? Where are you in your relationships? Single, married, with kids, divorced, stuck, content? Where are you with your body and your health? Strong and active or fighting a chronic disease or aging? God asks this question to us (along with Adam and Eve) in relation to him. "Where are you with me?" he asks. "Are you moving toward me or away from me? Are you in partnership or rebellion?" Today, right now, answer God's question to you: *where are you?*

## "WHO TOLD YOU THAT YOU WERE NAKED?"

### GEN. *3:11*

*Naked* is such an ugly word, such a stark word. I prefer words like *nude, natural, and unclothed. Naked* is the harsh word for warts and all. It's the word of embarrassed discovery. It describes something without makeup or presentation. *Naked* is vulnerable and cringing. It's what happened to many of us when our privacy was violated, and we slammed the door in fear. No one likes to be seen *naked!* We all have parts of us that we wish to cover or conceal. Genesis 2:25 describes the man and woman as *naked and not ashamed.* That's the way God meant us to be. But when sin entered the equation, *nakedness* was now yoked to *shame.*

*Naked* is the shame script that reminds us of what a failure and disappointment we are. *Naked* is the shame response we have when we cringe at being up front or in the scrutiny of others. We know that we don't measure up and that what we have is never good enough. Whose voice(s) told you that you were *naked?* Name them, confess them, and release them.

## "HAVE YOU EATEN FROM THE TREE THAT I COMMANDED YOU NOT TO EAT FROM?"

*GEN. 3:11*

It's a yes or no question. I hate those! I like to give justifications and rationales for why I did or did not do something. Actions need to be contextualized and framed to make sense. There are precedents and causes for why I did what I did. And before I say yes or no, I need to make a case for my conduct.

How cluttered are your answers to God's questions? How circuitous do you go in responding to God? How much, like Eve and Adam, do you blame others for your behavior? Did you?

**"WHAT IS THIS THAT YOU HAVE DONE?"**

*GEN. 3:13*

It's not that complicated of a question, yet it demands looking at the consequences of my behavior. For Adam and Eve, it was just a piece of fruit. No big deal, really. But it set in motion a relationship collapse that only Jesus could restore.

What are the consequences of your behavior? What are the repercussions of your words spoken to others? Do you know what your facial reaction does to others? Do you know what your generosity (or greediness) does to the body of Christ? What we do counts and matters, for good or for ill. What actions have you done (or refused to do) before reading these words today? Are you aware of the relationships into which God has placed your life that will be different because of what you do?

## "WHY ARE YOU SO ANGRY? WHY IS YOUR FACE DOWNCAST?"

*GEN. 4:5*

Anger is off limits. It's just an emotion, and I'm entitled to be as angry as I want to be. I really can't help it when I get angry. Someone says something, does something, and, boom, I'm angry! A car cuts me off, an appliance breaks, someone disappoints me, and I'm angry. In fact, some of us are all anger, all the time. Anger is our constant companion, ready to bubble up and spill over at a moment's notice. Our parents were angry. Our family was angry. Our neighborhood and community was angry. We participated in angry sports and angry politics. Our entertainment and music were angry. Why are we angry? What a dumb question: it's because everyone else is angry, and it's what we need to do to survive.

In the case of Cain, it had to do with a sacrifice being rejected in favor of a brother's. Oh yeah, that gets anger going. Rejection, hurt, disappointment, failure, entitlement—what gets you so angry? Touch the anger in yourself. Name it. Spin it around in front of your face and describe it. Give it to God.

**"WHERE IS YOUR BROTHER?"**

*GEN. 4:9*

Where is _____ anyway? Where are they now? What ever happened to _____? You know those conversations. They start up innocently enough. Someone notices someone else is missing—from church, from a group, from a family gathering—and people want to know. Where is she? And you know.

We all know where certain bodies are buried. We know what happened, what was said, and what was done. We took care of that problem person on our own, and they will not be back around to bother us anymore. In subtle—and not so subtle ways—we let it be known that they were "dead" to our group and could go find somewhere else. Kids do it and adults do it. And God wants to know where our brother or sister is now. Do you know?

## "What have you done?"

### *Gen. 4:10*

Cain skirted the truth and lied to God. He did not want to say where Abel was. He did not want to take responsibility for his brother's death. It was about his rejection and anger, not Abel. Abel brought it on himself by being so responsible, such a goody-two shoes! Abel could have prevented all this if he had simply shared what he knew about sacrifices God liked.

This simple, yet probing, question brings us to the hardest choice, to admit we were wrong, to admit we caused the hurt, to admit we sinned. What have you done recently that you grieve? What have you said that broke someone? Some of us don't even know it anymore. We are so busy justifying our conduct and being angry, we can't see the wake of hurt we create. Do you know what you've done?

## "WHERE IS YOUR WIFE SARAH?"

### GEN. 18:9

It was a silly idea and a promise that Abraham knew really could not happen. The physiology was just not there. It was a nice gesture on God's part to promise a child through Sarah, but she was really old. Abraham was older, but he performed. He did conceive a child through Hagar and that, in itself, was something. He was even kind of proud of the fact that he could indeed father a child at his age. The child, Ishmael, did cause some tension between Hagar & Sarah. But that was their problem. He had a son!

When the visitors asked about Sarah, it caught him off guard. What does anyone want Sarah for anymore? She had been a good wife and loyal partner, way beyond loyal, even giving him Hagar to bear a son. Why ask about Sarah now?

Who are your "Sarah's"? Who are those old promises that you've long given up on? Who are those people with whom you once had a spiritual relationship, but have now moved on and moved away from? Who are the old Sunday school teachers or counselors who were there for you long ago, but play no active role in your life today? Where are they?

"WHY DID SARAH LAUGH AND SAY, 'WILL I REALLY
HAVE A CHILD, NOW THAT I AM OLD?' IS ANYTHING
TOO HARD FOR THE LORD?"

*GEN. 18:13*

Think Sarah was surprised when she heard the news? I'm
glad I'm writing this at age 60. I'm a grandfather now. I know a
bit more about how the body works and doesn't work. I've seen
my body go through changes that come with age. My wife and
I are really comfortable with our bodies and lives at this stage of
life. We like having kids and grandkids around. But we also like
the silence of our routines now. The very thought of having and
raising a young child now; that's ridiculous! Crazy! No way!

What's off the table between you and God? What is no
longer a viable option for God to do in your life? Where have
you given up dreaming and simply accepted the harsh realities
of life in your body and place? Too many believers reign in all
the adventure and excitement over time and exchange it for
predictable routine. The new is turned in for the familiar. We
don't do unknown anymore; we stay with the tried and true. Are
there places that would be *too hard for the Lord?*

## "SHALL I HIDE FROM ABRAHAM WHAT I AM ABOUT TO DO?"

### GEN. *18:17*

This is a funny question. It's a question from God to himself. It's a painful question about amputation. It's a question about cancer treatment. It's a question about divorce or job termination. For God knew the evil of Sodom and Gomorrah had to be punished decisively. That's a fine concept to type and read, but, when it is acted out, people die and many suffer. God's righteousness takes sin and injustice very seriously. There will be judgment and punishment and it will hurt. And Abraham will not like it at all. But God answers his question in the affirmative and tells Abraham his plans. Abraham springs into action, interceding for the righteous remnant left in Sodom (thus rescuing Lot).

If you knew what God was going to do, what would you do about it?

## "WHAT IS THE MATTER HAGAR?"

### GEN. *21:17*

Ever been used? Have you given yourself to someone or some cause with your heart, soul and mind—only to get dumped? Do you know what it's like to work for an organization selflessly for years—only to be asked to step down or leave? Have you been in a relationship with someone and been betrayed, lied to, or rejected?

Hagar is a poster-child for a victim. She did not ask to get pregnant. She did not volunteer to bear old Abraham's child. She just worked for Sarah. Then she gave her body to her mistress' husband as an act of obedience. And now where was she? In the desert with her son, dying of starvation and thirst. Talk about betrayal!

And God wanted to know what was the matter. God wanted to know the details and inside story of this abused woman. God still wants to know what is the matter with us. Why are we so hurt, so stuck, so wounded?

## "WHAT IS YOUR NAME?"

### GEN. 32:27

Jacob was not a nice man. In fact, I don't really like Jacob. He was a momma's boy. He cheated on his brother twice. He lied to his father. He ran away from responsibility and consequences. He's not someone I'd like to befriend, work with, or trust. He is oily!

He flees to his uncle Laban, gets cheated by Laban, and marries his two daughters who fight all the time. Tensions rise between Jacob and Laban (no doubt!), and he decides to return and reconcile with Esau. But, even in that act, he is both deceptive and cowardly. He sends his servants, wives and children ahead of him to "soften" his brother with gifts (read: bribes). They could be killed in Esau's anger while he stayed safely behind!

All alone in the desert, with everyone and everything on the move toward Esau, an angel approaches him and asks his name. What do people call you? What do you call yourself? What would you like to be called? How are you known? What names do you like? What names do you hate? Are you: Boss, Dad, Mom, Honey, Hey You (!), Stupid, a cruel nickname, a meme—what's your name today?

## "WHY DO YOU ASK MY NAME?"

### *GEN. 32:29*

Jacob told the angel his name and was re-named a most accurate name: Israel, meaning he struggled with God. In the emptiness of the desert, that name both described and blessed Jacob. He was a struggler and a fighter, a conniver and a provocateur. But being a struggler, he wanted to know who he was dealing with, what is *your* name? And the angel asked him, "Why?" Why do he want to know? What was his aim in knowing the name of an angel? Did he want to cash it in for something? Did he want to use it for his own purpose? (Can you see I still don't trust Jacob?)

The angel did not give Jacob (Israel) his name; rather, he blessed him namelessly. How about you? Do you want to know the names, details, and facts? Or are you willing to be blessed namelessly? Are you a spiritual name-dropper who likes to let others know who and what you know? Or are you a weary desert wanderer, a struggler with God who is content with a blessing in the night?

### "WHAT IS IN YOUR HAND?"

*EXOD. 4:2*

There are few more reluctant leaders than Moses. He is a pastor's role model for being dragged kicking and screaming into service for God. In his first encounter with God, he argued with God five times about why he should not be the one to go to Pharaoh and work for the release of the Jews. He has endless reasons why God made a mistake in choosing him for this.

Ever argue with God? Have you ever been sure that what you think God wants you to do is unreasonable and stupid? When you hear calls for volunteers and helpers for ministries, have you ever said to yourself, "No way! That's not going to happen with me!"? As I read through the Bible for this study, I found only one volunteer: David facing Goliath. It seems like everyone else God uses, he called from a position of reluctance.

And God asked Moses what he was holding, what was in his hand? The answer was obvious: the tool of his trade—a shepherd's staff. It was the only thing Moses used day in and day out. It was attached to his hand, smoothed by his grip. And God used it dramatically by turning it into a serpent, a conveyor of plagues, causing water partings, and water gushings. What are you holding in your hand today? What goes with you everywhere? If you throw it on the ground like Moses did, what might God do with it?

**"Who gave humans their mouths? Who makes them deaf or mute? Who gives them sight or makes them blind? Is it not I, the Lord?"**

*Exod. 4:11*

"I don't sing!" is a common response grumpy people make to me about worship. They stand with their arms folded across their chests, waiting for the music (which they don't usually like) to be over so they can sit down and hear a sermon. When asked to offer prayer, these ones will often respond, "I don't pray out loud," and refuse to pray. When asked to give a witness to God in their lives, the response is, "I'm not comfortable speaking in public; ask someone else." Oh, I know those answers. I've heard them hundreds of times over the years. And those answers are lies. Why?

Because I've seen them with their grandchildren, making silly faces, spouting gibberish, and singing nursery songs. I've seen them eloquently articulate why a certain athlete, politician or celebrity should be valued. And I've been with a number of them at sporting events when they cheered like crazy when their team scored.

The question God asked Moses was about sovereignty and control. Who really made and controls the mouths and eyes of people: God or us? In what way will you dare to let God use your mouth today?

## "WHAT ABOUT YOUR BROTHER, AARON THE LEVITE?"

### *EXOD. 4:14*

We are still dealing with Moses in this question. Moses steadfastly objects to God's plan to use him. He is sure God is making a huge mistake. He is reluctant, petulant and frightened. He tried to help out the Jews once, long ago, and that backfired terribly. So much so that he had to run for his life. Moses was not going back there ever again, and he told God all the reasons why he would not work.

But then God gets creative, strategic, and (do I dare say?) dirty! *What about your brother?* What about my brother? Didn't you want me, Lord? Isn't this really about you and me? Why get my brother involved? What does he have to do with this?

The problem that most of us Western believers face is that we do ministry alone. We decide alone. We act alone. We dream and plan alone. We go alone. We witness alone. We get others around us to help with *our* plans. And the end result is exhausted, burned-out believers (see Exodus 18). Look at the way Jesus used disciples in the Gospels and how the church grew in Acts (hint: partnerships, two-by-two, going out together).

What about you today? Who's going with you? What about your brother (or sister) _____? Who do you invite (ask or plead) to go with you into ministry and service? How long will you keep doing this alone?

## "How long will you refuse to humble

## yourself before me?"

*Exod. 10:3*

Moses has been in a power struggle with Pharaoh for seven plagues: blood, frogs, gnats, flies, livestock illness, boils, and hail. So, before the locusts and the last plague of the death of all firstborn sons, God asked Pharaoh a question through Moses. It's the question of truth to power. *When will you humble yourself before God?* Or, rather, it's about how long will you *refuse* the act of humbling yourself?

It's the problem parents face with all two year olds who have learned the power they have in the word *NO*. Little children find the power in asserting their independence and love saying NO to authority about picking up, nap times, eating, sharing, you name it! It's a huge challenge, when we live among authorities we do not like, and we refuse to humble ourselves before them. One writer recently said that the one word everyone in our culture universally hates is the word *submit*. No one likes to submit: children don't, young people don't, men certainly don't, and women absolutely don't. Middle-aged adults don't even think about it. Senior adults bristle at the thought of it. The wealthy and powerful don't even think about doing it. And the poor and disenfranchised resent it daily.

Yet, God asks Pharaoh, Moses, Aaron and us, "How long will you refuse to humble yourself *before me*?" What would that look like in your skin today? What would humility look like in your neighborhood and social circles? Pharaoh learned the hard way—must we?

## "Why are you crying out to me?"

### Exod. 14:15

In a part of a book I wrote, called "Sacred Time/Sacred Space," I described sacred leadership as always "leadership from the middle." Sacred leadership is always conferred leadership and not inherent or entitled leadership. God grants it and God takes it away. Sacred leadership serves the plans and needs of God, not us. That's a pain! That means sacred leaders are always stuck in the middle somewhere between where God wants them to go and where the people they lead refuse to go.

In this part of Exodus, the leadership of Moses from the middle is painfully clear: the Red Sea looms in front of the people, Pharaoh's army and chariots are pounding up behind them, and the people complain. What's going on Moses? Are you trying to kill us? Is this your idea of a good plan—either drown or get slaughtered? Moses replied with the powerful call not to fear, but to stand firm, to see the Lord's deliverance, simply to be still.

That's really good theology, but something is missing in the text between when Moses said that to the people and the question above in vs. 15. Moses must have had a meltdown with God. Unloading his fears and complaints to God about the people he leads, the conditions around them, and even God's own timing.

Oh, that's so me! I love being a pastor but can so quickly resent the people I'm called to lead. I get hurt by their criticisms and frustrated by their slowness. My prayers don't get answered soon enough, and God's plans seem to have major holes in them. And so I cry, complain, whine, and brood. And God asks of me *why are you crying out to me?* My job is to lead and to move ahead, not to complain. That's what Moses did, and the sea parted and the people escaped and the armies drowned. What next step beyond crying is God asking you to take?

## "Is the Lord's arm too short"?

### *Num. 11:23*

As a new believer I read straight through the Bible while I was out of the country for a year in Japan. Midway through Numbers (maybe around here) I gave up on the people of Israel and thought God made a bad investment. These people just did not get it. They were rebellious, selfish, surly, and contentious. I mean God dramatically freed them from slavery, continually provided food, water, protection, and guidance, yet the people's response was more complaining. The latest version of complaining was the romantic fantasy about how wonderful life was back in great, old Egypt! Those were the good old days. Nothing like slavery! It would be as crazy as former slaves longingly thinking about plantation living and all the great cornbread and collard greens!

God's plan was laid out in verses 16 and 17, in gathering leaders around Moses to share the burden of leadership that was buckling him. God would take some of the power of the Spirit and spread it around, lightening the load. To that Moses objected. How would it work? Who would be qualified after he had been doing this for so long? The people would not accept anyone else...blah, blah, blah!

This is the bottom-line question for us: can God address our situation? Can he actually do anything about what we are going through? Is his arm too short?

## "WHY THEN WERE YOU NOT AFRAID TO SPEAK AGAINST MY SERVANT MOSES?"

*NUM. 12:8*

Moses was a less-than-perfect leader. Nobody knew that better than his closest associates (and family), Miriam and Aaron. They saw his weaknesses up close. They were familiar with his rants and outbursts. They knew what a poor communicator he was, especially compared to Aaron. He even married poorly. (A Cushite for goodness sake! What kind of pastor's wife would a Cushite make?) And they grumbled to others about their disappointment in Moses' leadership abilities. Maybe within those criticisms was the seed that they could do better as a two-person team (just speculation).

I'm good at complaining about leaders. I'm astute at seeing mistakes that leaders around me make, ones that I certainly would not make. As a local church pastor I am especially prone to criticize conference and denominational leaders who "just don't seem to get" the realities of local church life, since they live in an ivory tower of bureaucracy.

And I know church members and staff complain about me. After serving four churches over thirty years, I know most of the complaints about my personality and leadership style pretty well. And, they are right. I'm a flawed and broken person, often reluctantly serving God and complaining about the people I'm called to lead.

But God has other plans for us who serve under leaders: *are we not afraid to speak against his servant* _____*?* (You can fill in the blank about the leader you complain about most). What are we to do about leaders whose faults we see too clearly? Let's not complain…but pray.

"HOW LONG WILL THESE PEOPLE TREAT ME WITH
CONTEMPT? HOW LONG WILL THEY REFUSE TO
BELIEVE IN ME, IN SPITE OF ALL THE SIGNS I HAVE
PERFORMED AMONG THEM?"

*NUM. 14:11*

I used to love to wander new car lots. There was a particular brand and model I wanted to purchase, but could not commit. Each time I came, the same salesman, Gary, would walk with me through the lot, talking about features and prices of various cars. We always came back to the same model, and I would hesitate and walk away. This went on for months. One day Gary burst out: "Okay, Mr. Johnson, I know you want this car; what's it going to take on my part to get you to buy it?" What's it going to take? My wife and I talked about payment amounts and trade-in value, and I shared it with Gary, and he met it. But then I faced a crisis: would I take the next step and buy the car? I did, and it was one of the best cars we ever owned!

The people of Israel were addicted to grumbling. It was their mother tongue. No one knew how to complain and grumble better than these people. Their default behavior in the face of any change or event was complaint and grumbling. It was their language and their entitlement. Moses and Aaron were both wearied by it and worried about it. They worried that the constant state of grumbling would not only postpone, but also possibly jeopardize, God's promise of a new land.

*How long* is a painful question from God to us. How long will we treat God shabbily and refuse to believe and trust him after all he has done for us? How long will it be before we actually tithe ten percent? How long will it be before we forgive our enemy? How long will it be before we let go of our anger and resentments? How long will it be before we let God control our tongues? How long?

## "WHO ARE THESE MEN WITH YOU?"

### NUM. 22:9

*"Can we have lunch sometime, pastor?"* is always followed up in my mind with the question: *about what?* When someone asks for lunch out of the blue, there is almost always an agenda. And, when I arrive at the lunch spot and find two more people, my defenses go up immediately. One of the consequences of being a pastor is being lobbied, not unlike school principals, mayors, elected representatives, or anyone in a position of authority. And that is not always bad. I need to have my eyes opened to realities I don't always see. I need logic presented to me about situations unclear to me. I even need to know who is behind and supportive of initiatives.

Balaam was in just such a position. He was a spiritual guy who had the ability to invoke blessings and curses. He did it professionally (read: for a fee). The king of the region, Balaak, and his leaders were really worried about this traveling nation called Israel. They were sure it would eat them out of house and home. So instead of negotiating safe passage with them, they opted to get Balaam to curse them. But Balaam insisted on talking with God about this first, and God asked this question: w*ho are these men with you?* Who is bringing this concern? What do their lives represent? How are they faithful people? How does their agenda mesh with mine?

That's a real question for every one of us as we begin a day, knowing we will be approached, lobbied, and urged to take a position, to act on something, to pronounce something. Who are these people with us, surrounding us, influencing us? Are they on God's side? Should we really be listening to them as much are we are?

## "WHY HAVE YOU BEATEN YOUR DONKEY THESE THREE TIMES?"

*NUM. 22:32*

Balaam was a poor listener to God and much more influenced by local power and money. He caved in to pressure from those he knew, and he rode off to curse the Israelites on a donkey (I appreciate the older translation of donkey as an "ass," which makes the animal more silly). But God intervened through the donkey. The donkey balked and rammed Balaam into a wall to avoid getting cut in two by an angel with a sword (that the donkey saw and Balaam didn't). Balaam did what any of us would do—he hauled off and smacked the donkey—not once, but three times.

Ever had something foil your plans like a car breakdown, a tech problem, or some sort of malfunction? What did you do? What I do is boil over and fume at the stupid _____! I have been known to toss objects across the room that did not work as I thought they should. But could it be that God used those breakdowns, failures, and system collapses to get my attention just like he did with Balaam's donkey?

So today, when something doesn't go right and does not meet your demands, what will you do? Beat it or thank God for it?

**"HAVE I NOT COMMANDED YOU? BE STRONG AND COURAGEOUS.
DO NOT BE AFRAID; DO NOT BE DISCOURAGED, FOR THE LORD
YOUR GOD WILL BE WITH YOU WHEREVER YOU GO."**
*JOSH. 1:9*

I don't always want to be strong, courageous, not afraid, or not discouraged. I want to be liked. I want to be popular. I want others to say nice things about me and invite me to their parties. I want to run from challenges and battles and have long cups of coffee with good friends on sunny days. I like to avoid tough decisions and blame others for my problems.

Young Joshua was now in command. Old Moses was dead, and it was his turn to step into the leadership role he had observed for many years. And Joshua was not naïve. He knew the battles Moses fought and the obstacles and resistance to his leadership. This was not going to be a picnic. Solid leadership never is.

The future has never been so daunting as it is now. There have never been more uncertainties about more things as we face this part of the 21st century. Trends from the past are poor indicators of the future challenges before us. The maps have changed. They landscape is new. We've never been here before. This is not the old wilderness, but a new land. Go back to your call. Go back to your salvation. Whose are you? Who has called you and commanded you? And, more importantly, who is with you right now today?

## "STAND UP! WHAT ARE YOU DOING

### DOWN ON YOUR FACE?"

*JOSH. 7:10*

The first test of Joshua's leadership (under God and for the people of Israel) was a splendid success. They stopped the waters of the Jordan and marched down the walls of Jericho. It worked just like God promised! Joshua was on a roll with God. Success can be a heady thing.

The second test didn't go so well. The Israelites marched up to face the smaller city of Ai with less than 3,000 men instead of the whole army. This should take an afternoon at most. But soon everything went south. The opposition was fierce; the Israelites balked and were chased away.

Nothing teaches good leadership better than splendid failure. All the starch was knocked out of Joshua's shirts. His plans failed and everyone knew it. In leadership, you are only as good as your last battle, and Joshua was a failure. So he tore his clothes, fell on his face before the Ark of the Covenant, and covered himself with ashes. He was busted and broken and ready.

When God calls us from face down to face up, then we are ready for new and deeper lessons about following God. The plan didn't fail; the people did (specifically the solider named Achan who stole goods he should not have). The obstacle (not enemy)

Joshua had to face was obedience within his ranks. It was not about the enemies out there but disobedience in here.

Where is your world face down? Where are your former great plans nothing but piles of ashes? Where are you most bewildered and confused? Confess it; then listen for God's voice.

" '…YOU SHALL NOT MAKE A COVENANT WITH THE PEOPLE
OF THIS LAND, BUT YOU SHALL BREAK DOWN THEIR ALTARS.'
YET YOU HAVE DISOBEYED ME. WHY HAVE YOU DONE THIS?"

*JUDG. 2:2*

"Let's make a deal" is the story of our lives. In order to get along in society, we have to make deals, compromises, and truces. The marketplace of life demands give and take. Asking prices are seldom selling prices. It's just the way things are. I've been there (and still am there in some areas). There are some things just not worth the fight: media violence, sex as advertising, consumer greed, ignorance of the poor, racism, etc. As we grow older, we just learn to live with it. We ignore prejudicial comments from old friends and tolerate the abuse of vulnerable ones. It's just too much work to be on the battle lines all the time.

Settling the land of Israel was tough work. Kicking out (or killing) the people already there was tougher than working out deals and compromises. You get this land; we'll take that. I'll give you my son for your daughter. I'll buy from you if you buy from me. It's the marketplace of life. But for how far and to what length? How far have we compromised being people of Jesus for being good citizens and neighbors? What deals have we made to be accepted and belong instead of being sold out wholly for God? What deals have you made that need a good once over? Go over them with God.

## "AM I NOT SENDING YOU?"

### *JUDG. 6:14*

"Oh no, not him!" I told the Lord when this young man told me that he was going to be a pastor. He just did not have what it took to be a pastor. He would get ground up and spit out. He came from a dysfunctional family. He was pathologically shy. He was physically awkward. He was naively sincere. Oh Lord, not him! So I did my pastoral best to dissuade him from ministry toward something safer, something more routine and reliable. But he would not be dissuaded. His teachers discouraged him and his peers doubted him. But he would not let go of the dream.

Now he has been pastoring successfully for many years in a small church. They love him like they've never loved another pastor. And he loves them and can think of no place better to be than where he is.

Nobody would ever choose Gideon: little, least, lowest, and last. His skill set? He threshed wheat in a wine vat for fear of neighboring gangs. His tribe and family were on the "never to invite" list of outliers and marginal. And the thing is, Gideon knew all this and accepted it. His goal in life was to get to sundown alive, that's all, just survive.

Until an angel of God came along and disrupted his mediocre life with a call: "The Lord is with you mighty warrior!" (Judg.

6:12) When all is said and done, it's all about faithfulness to the call. Classes, seminars, coaching, and mentoring are helpful, but only the call is sustaining over the long haul. Call is not volunteering, but obeying—even reluctantly. Where is God sending you?

## "DID I NOT SAVE YOU FROM THEIR HANDS?"

### JUDG. 10:12

Do you know your history? Can you narrate your spiritual journey? Can you locate those times of faithfulness and those times of unfaithfulness? How about beyond your individual story to that of your family? Who was the faith leader in your family of origin? Where were those places of commitment and obedience? Where did they fail and bail on God? How about grandparents? What did you learn about God by watching your grandparents? What price did they pay to follow God or what price did they pay for ignoring God?

We are a studiously ahistorical culture. Our history starts and stops with me and goes no further back than this week. We are constantly buying the myth that we can re-invent ourselves and retool our identities. The result is our current, shallow culture that has no real memory or history. Not so with God's people. God relentlessly and painfully reminds the people of Israel of their grumbling and failure, of their faithlessness and adultery to other gods, other faiths, and other myths. But God also reminded the people of his faithfulness to redeem them after they confessed and repented and called out to him.

This question is posed by God to a currently wayward and rebellious people, who were *doing evil in the sight of the Lord* (Judg.

to remove the boys (who loved the house and all the perks) and find a faithful servant to replace Eli.

So God asked Eli the question above. The word that jumps out is *clearly*. What about God's standards and requirements were *not clear*? How did God lower his standards for being a priest to accommodate selfish boys? When I get all caught up in my sense of entitlement, this is a question to ask. We can also go further and ask, where does Jesus promise (fill in the blank with the thing you are currently fussing about) when he invited you to take up your cross and follow him?

**"Why do you scorn my sacrifice and offering that I prescribed for my dwelling? Why do you honor your sons more than me by fattening yourselves on the choice parts of every offering made by my people Israel?"**

*1 Sam. 2:29*

Eli was a good father. Eli loved his boys with all his heart. Eli could only see the good things about these boys. He would do anything for their happiness and success. Eli was like many parents today. When I grew up, if I received a "D" or an "F" grade, my parents blamed me for not doing the work. Today, if students receive "D's" or "F's," they prepare themselves to be assaulted by parents who demand better grades and criticize the teacher for daring to treat their child so contemptuously!

The painful question behind the question here is: do you worship your children and family more than God? *Why do you honor your sons more than me* is an awful, painful question. I love my children. I would do almost anything for them. Do I worship them more than God? Do I lower spiritual standards for my children and family to keep them happy? How far do we go in compromising God for family?

## "HOW LONG WILL YOU MOURN FOR SAUL, SINCE I HAVE REJECTED HIM AS KING OVER ISRAEL?"

*1 SAM. 16:1*

It was over. King Saul knew it and Samuel knew it. Saul lost God's anointing power and favor. For all sorts of reasons, Saul abandoned God for his status and power as king, and God withdrew his spirit from him. However, Samuel loved Saul. Samuel was the priest who anointed Saul as first king over Israel. Saul was, in essence, Samuel's project and prodigy. God's rejection of Saul was, in a sense, a rejection and reflection on Samuel. If only he could have done better, maybe this would have not happened.

It's painful in a pastorate over long years to realize that the current problem facing you in ministry was one of your former solutions. The first years in a church are relatively easy because all the problems were those of your predecessor, and you are certainly *not* like him/her! But, over time, a church or an organization or even a family needs to change and adapt and let go of the past out of faithfulness to God.

The question is *how long will you mourn* over that which God has rejected and called you away from? How long will you mourn the *good old days* that were never that good? How long will you mourn

_____? The solution? The answer? Get over it! What are you still mourning that you need to get over? How long?

## "ARE YOU THE ONE TO BUILD ME A HOUSE TO DWELL IN?"

### 2 SAM. 7:5

King David made things happen. He was a man after God's own heart. He was brave and fearless (read about Goliath). He worshiped God with abandon. He was both passionate (dangerously so with Bathsheba) and repentant. He got things done. He faced down enemies and brokered treaties with neighbors. He was good for business and became personally wealthy and successful. He built and built! King David attracted success. He helped build a nation, an economy, and a reputation.

Now he wanted to build a house for God that equaled or surpassed his own palace. He had the energy, the funds, and the will to build a great thing for God. He could make a new megachurch of all megachurches!

When people come to me with willingness, a plan, and resources to do something big for God, I'm usually all in on that! I love riding the coattails of success. And so did Samuel. Sounded like a good idea from a good man, from God's man. Then God asked the question to David though Samuel: *are you the one to build me a house?* Why not? There would be too much blood, too much violence. God wanted someone else to build what David planned. God would not allow an aggressive and powerful King to box him in. God was mobile and agile and not confined. Just because David could, did not mean he should. Where does God ask you: *are you the one?*

## "WHAT ARE YOU DOING HERE, ELIJAH?"

### *1 KINGS 19:9, 13*

I like it when questions are asked twice. Sometimes on the first go-round, the question is asked and answered in a perfunctory and functional way. Elijah has been carrying the entire spiritual load of Israel on his shoulders for years (or at least months). He predicted drought due to faithlessness (I Kings 17); he was fed by ravens; he was cared for by a widow and raised her dead son; he fought with the 450 prophets of Baal; he confronted the king; and now he was running for his life from the king's angry and powerful wife Jezebel. He was exhausted, frayed, disappointed, and done. He spent all the "chips" he had, but it still wasn't good enough. So, when God asks him the first time what he was doing here (in the desert under a bush), Elijah is ready with a long complaint about his faithfulness and the people's faithlessness. And he wants to quit. God invited him to experience God all over again from the crevice of a rock as *he passed by* (I Kings 19:11). That's when Elijah experienced the *still, small voice of God* asking him the same question: *what are you doing here?*

If you are reading this, I can make the assumption that you have been attempting to be a faithful servant of Jesus for some years. You have tried and trusted, and you have failed and been disappointed. Serving God over the long haul is an endurance run that exhausts the strongest of believers. And for many of us, the longer we serve, the more solo we become. We carry the load by ourselves. We trust fewer people because we've been let down too many times. We're suspicious of the most sincere church people because we've been betrayed by friends. We easily become cynical of the latest initiatives and programs and leaders from headquarters because we've seen them come and go before. We know the flip charts and the models for successful churchmanship. And it always seems to come down to us having to do more. That's it Lord; I'm done!

And God re-called Elijah to a new ministry of leadership appointment and mentoring of the young Elisha to take his mantle of leadership. How are you being re-called by God from your place of legitimate exhaustion? Where is the young Elisha whom God is calling you to invite along? We are not as alone as we feel.

## "Have you not noticed how Ahab has humbled himself before me?"

### *1 Kings 21:29*

Ahab is not a cuddly character. He is not the role model for faithful kings of Israel. He married wicked queen Jezebel and was compromised by all of her Baal priests. He was a survival bureaucrat, who did what he had to do to stay in power. He was a user and manipulator. Nope, he was not a cuddly kind of king.

We all know those types—hard-driving executives who always arrive at meetings pressed and powerful looking, who give orders rather than ask questions, who drop names of important people they know, who always one-up any conversation, and who are the heroes to their own stories. They can be men or women, young or old. They exude power and bluster and the desire to be in control.

But this time, Ahab repented of his sin of stealing a vineyard from a man by having him unjustly killed (Naboth in I Kings 21) and admitted his sin to Elisha. Did Elisha believe it? No. This was just one more ploy, one more act of a chameleon leader trying to get out of trouble. But God saw differently and asked Elisha to see the genuineness of Ahab's repentance.

There are some I have a hard time seeing repentance. There are some to whom I have a hard time giving another chance.

There are some who are now on my list of not-to-trust-ever-again. And the danger is that I will not be God's instrument when they do repent because I won't give them another chance. Who have you noticed is humbling him/herself like never before? Will you give them grace?

## "WHY DO YOU DISOBEY THE LORD'S COMMANDS?"

### 2 CHRON. 24:20

The people of Israel were in outright rebellion against God. They abandoned Temple worship. They erected Asherah poles and worshiped at them (fertility rites) and crafted idols for personal use. I mean, this is bad stuff. So God sent prophets, many prophets, to them to call them back to faithfulness, but they refused to hear them.

The reward went to Zechariah, the prophet of God, to go back to the people with this question: *why do you disobey the Lord's commands?* Why is disobedience so attractive? Why is the impulse to resist God so strong in our hearts? Why does submission to authority rankle us and get us so angry? Where does that come from?

The question really goes to me first. I have read God's Word many, many times. I know what God likes and dislikes. I know what God wants from me. I know what it means to be a follower of Jesus. I know what God expects from me as a husband, father, grandfather, and pastor. Yet still I buck; still I resist. What's with that? What's the attraction of disobedience in your life? Today, ask God to flag every moment of disobedience and ask *why?*

## "WHERE HAVE YOU COME FROM?"

### JOB 1:7, 2:2

As a little boy, I would sometimes belch a loud burp, and my mother or father would look at me and ask, "Where did that come from?" They were surprised that such a loud noise could come rolling out of me. I try now, as an adult, to control belching behavior, but the question remains: *where did that come from?*

Job is not a fun book to read. It's a book full of deep suffering and good friends' good advice yielding frustrating responses. It's a book that draws the reader to the edge of the mystery of suffering and righteousness and why good people go through bad things. At the beginning of the book, Satan shows up before God, and God asks him a question: *where have you come from?* And the answer to God's question is **Hell**. Satan comes from no good place—though he will not admit it.

In studying conflict resolution, I was advised to ask three questions when someone brought a complaint about another person to me. One: have you talked with the other person about your concern? Two: can I go with you to the other person so we can talk together? Three: If you have neither talked directly to the other person and do not want me to go with you to him/her, what is your intention? *Where are you coming from?*

Everything has a precedent. Something is always before. Every one of us comes from some other place before we are here right now. Can you name, identify and confess where you have come from? Where have you come from in your inner life? What's been happening with your family and personal identity? Tell God where you have come from today.

## "HAVE YOU CONSIDERED MY SERVANT JOB?"
### *Job 1:8, 2:3*

This question bothers me. It's like God volunteering Job for active combat without asking his permission. When Satan accused God of manipulation, getting people to love him by giving them nice things, God offered up Job as a guinea pig. Thanks, God! You know the rest of the story. Job gets utterly stripped of his family, wealth and health. But he will not curse God; instead he submits, "The Lord gave and the Lord has taken away; may the name of the Lord be praised." (Job 1:21)

Rev. Charles Hackett was the Assembly of God pastor in Lafayette, Indiana, when I first began ministry. He was my mentor and good friend. One day in his deep Indiana twang he said to me, "Don, where there's light, there's bugs!" and with that he told me to expect spiritual assaults for being faithful. It comes with the territory.

Faithfulness to God is not a protection from, rather an invitation for, attack. Our current obsession with safety is found nowhere in scripture. Could God again be saying *Have you considered my servant_____?*

## "WHERE WERE YOU WHEN I LAID THE FOUNDATIONS OF THE EARTH?"

### JOB 38:4

One of the things my wife and I love to do together in France is drive, especially into the mountains north of us. They are not mountains like the Rocky Mountains but more like the Appalachian Mountains. Highways are cut through the rocks and expose deep seams and striations that angle one way or another. These seams often glisten with different sediments or black coal. It makes me wonder, how did that get there? When were these levels laid down? How did they get pushed up in this direction and at that angle? And I feel very small when I consider the foundations of the earth around me, but I am also invited to feel cared for by the same God who laid foundations and pushed up levels of earth millions of year ago. He cares for you.

"HAVE YOU GIVEN ORDERS TO THE MORNING OR
SHOWN THE DAWN ITS PLACE?"

*JOB 38:12*

How does time run for you? Are you consistently early or always late? Are you aware of the time or ignorant of what time it is now? Do you wear a watch or go by your instinct? Are you inspired by the dark of the early morning, or do you luxuriate in the waxing light of a sunset? Are you in a hurry or relaxed? Is time your friend, or is it a dreaded enemy? Do you enjoy what's happening to you as you age (mature!), or are your fighting it and fearing it?

How we handle time is a great indicator of how we trust God. Notice I did not say how we manage or control time. We don't manage it or control it nearly as much as we might think we do. Time is God's gift to us. It's his completely, totally. How can you rest in God's time today?

**"HAVE YOU JOURNEYED TO THE SPRINGS OF THE
SEA OR WALKED IN THE RECESSES OF THE DEEP?"**

*JOB 38:16*

I like to swim in the ocean in Santa Barbara. When I first started swimming, I wore goggles. I stopped that very quickly. Why? Because on days when the water was clear, I saw too much! I saw too many moving objects I could not identify. I saw huge schools of fish I did not know were there. And I imagined all the things that could swim up and grab me. So I stowed the goggles away and now swim basically sightless, only seeing things on the surface, or just below the surface.

How deep do you go in life? How deeply do you see below the surface of your daily living? Some of us prefer to do as I do in the ocean and remain blind to what lies beneath us. We don't want to see what's down there in the deeps. In the Old Testament, the deep places were the places where mystery resided and originated.

Like Job, most of us have not been to the really deep places in the oceans or in life. But God has been there. The deeps belong to him.

**"WHAT IS THE WAY TO THE ABODE OF LIGHT? AND WHERE DOES DARKNESS RESIDE?"**

*JOB 38:19*

How much do you love sunny days? How much are you affected by daylight or the lack of it? The condition called SAD (Seasonally Affective Disorder) was a big deal when we lived in Minnesota and Michigan, where sunlit days in the winter were sometimes weeks apart, and many days were filled with a slate gray sky and cold weather. We craved natural light! Living in California has made us insensitive to the value and beauty of light. We take it for granted—until it rains for a few days, and everyone wants to fly to Hawaii!

And how about sunsets? Where you live, are they slow and gradual or instant like a light switch? Does the sky linger with the afterglow of a sunset, or does it go immediately dark? Is darkness something you look forward to as an indicator of the end of the workday and time to be home to rest and sleep? Or is darkness a fear and an unknown?

The entire light spectrum belongs to God. Look for God today in the brilliantly bright places and in the places that are pitch dark.

## "DO YOU KNOW THE LAWS OF THE HEAVENS?"

### JOB 38:33

In 1977, Voyager I was launched into space. It has now gone beyond Jupiter and Pluto. It is, according to the Smithsonian Institute, 124 times further from the sun that we are (ninety-three million miles). It is three times further from us than Pluto. By 2025, it should penetrate the outer distance of our solar system and into another realm.

Astronomers and astrophysicists give me a headache when they plot these kinds of numbers and graphs about the universe. Beyond and beyond and beyond it goes. Is there life? Are the laws of physics and math universal or heliocentric? How far is far? If there is an end, what is on the other side of the end? God.

## "WILL ANYONE WHO CONTENDS WITH THE ALMIGHTY CORRECT HIM?"

*JOB 40:2*

I received a parking ticket some time ago. The ticket said I overstayed my allotted seventy-five minutes in the space. When I looked at the time stamp on the ticket, the infraction was impossible! I was still in a meeting on the other side of town and had witnesses. So I contested my ticket to the scoffing of my friends. "You'll never win," they said. I sent in my fine along with a letter of protest. And three months later, I received a check from the city along with an apology from the city for their error. How often does that happen? Rarely! But that's not to say that we do not witness or experience injustice or unfairness. We do all the time. But we weigh which battles are worth fighting.

God invites Job into the "courtroom" of heaven to contend with him. But contending is not the same as correcting. Contending declares a perceived injustice, while correcting places fault on the other party. Who are you contending with today? Who are you correcting?

## "WOULD YOU DISCREDIT MY JUSTICE? WOULD YOU CONDEMN ME TO JUSTIFY YOURSELF?"

*JOB 40:8*

We practice a strange relational math: *the enemy of my enemy is my friend* we say and practice. If you hate my enemy, we must have something in common because we both hate the same enemy. Really? Couldn't my enemy's enemy also be my enemy? Not if my sole aim is to justify my conduct. If I play out my life always attempting to win and to be right, I will make my enemy's enemy my friend in order to win and come out ahead.

The question behind this question is *how far will we take that?* Will our need to justify ourselves and appear right go so far as to discredit God's justice? How much do we need to be right in our own eyes, and how hard is it to be wrong? In the late Bruce Larson's book *There's a Lot More to Health than not being Sick*, he has a chapter titled "Do you want to be Right or be Well?" For many of us, we need to be right at all costs. What would it cost your life today to put aside your need to justify yourself, your conduct, your motives, and your actions?

## "YOU ASKED, 'WHO IS THIS THAT OBSCURES MY PLANS WITHOUT KNOWLEDGE?'"

### *JOB 42:3*

Obfuscation is easier than clarification. My father once told me a joke about how pastors can get out of arguments: *when in doubt, obfuscate!* It works. When someone "traps" me in a question I can't answer, I can always appeal to ancient Hebrew or Greek manuscripts to make things more confusing and more complex. That happens in meetings all the time. Someone doesn't like the direction a group is going, so he or she deflects attention with minutia and petty rules and regulations.

Do we ever do that with God—obscure his plans without knowledge? I think we do it all the time. When God's word clearly tells us to pray for our enemies, we find loopholes so we can pay them back. When God's word calls us to tithe and live generously, we invent all sorts of excuses for our greediness and stinginess. When God's Word tells us to practice love, we obscure his plans with our fears and hatred. Where could you be obscuring God's plans without knowledge?

## "WHEN THE FOUNDATIONS ARE BEING DESTROYED, WHAT CAN THE RIGHTEOUS DO?"

### Ps. 11:3

Foundations are not supposed to be destroyed. Foundations are supposed to endure and remain strong. Foundations are supposed to be established on firm footing so they do not shift and alter over time. But few human foundations remain forever. Cultures and civilizations that seemed invincible at one time (Egypt, Babylon, Assyria, Persia, Rome) expanded then crumbled. Leaders, political parties, and corporations seem invincible at their highest heights, but then they collapse or morph or fade. Institutions and even denominations rise up and then fade away. Human foundations do not last.

What can the righteous do during times of shifting and collapsing? Worship. God is in his holy Temple. God endures, remains, and abides. Don't be alarmed when foundations crack; God does not.

## "DO I EAT THE FLESH OF BULLS OR DRINK THE BLOOD OF GOATS?"

### Ps. 50:13

We are impressed with spectacle. Whether it is the inauguration of a new pope or president, or sports finals, we love the ceremony around recognition. And as a pastor, I know the draw and pull of being up front and having long prayers and fancy words. I love flowing robes full of symbolism and imagery. I love elaborate decorations and subtle touches of beauty.

Nobody had better liturgical practices than the Jews. The Old Testament gave them elaborate and specific instructions for sacrifices and offerings. There were ranks of Levites present to make sure things were done in just the right way. There was proper clothing and music, equipment and posture. It was pretty complicated but also pretty cool! Who does not get excited at a grand celebration when the jets fly overhead streaming red, white, and blue smoke? We are impressed. But is God?

Look at your personal rituals and routines. Are they for God or for you? Does God really need the fancy Thanksgiving meal or the elaborate Christmas gifts? Does your newest outfit or your most fancy toys impress God?

**"WHAT RIGHT HAVE YOU TO RECITE MY LAWS OR
TAKE MY COVENANT ON YOUR LIPS?"**

*Ps. 50:16*

God does not play games, and God is not fooled. I'm fooled often. I'm fooled most by well crafted and excellently delivered words. I can be moved to tears by a great singer and a sacred song. Sometimes, though, I'm the one doing the fooling. I'm the one playing "Mr. Religious" or "Mr. Righteous." I know the words and phrases. I can craft an eloquent public prayer. I know how to dress for the occasion and can put on a serious and important look. But, is God impressed? What right do I have to use God's words or recite his laws? None! It's all grace, not right or entitlement, or position. Get over yourself!

**"HOW LONG WILL YOU WHO ARE SIMPLE LOVE YOUR SIMPLE WAYS? HOW LONG WILL MOCKERS DELIGHT IN MOCKERY AND FOOLS HATE KNOWLEDGE?"**

*PROV. 1:22*

There was a silly movie out years ago called *Dumb and Dumber*. In it, two idiots traveled from mishap to mishap, making bad things worse than the audience could imagine. We laugh at the movie but cringe at real life. Are the simple doomed to being simple? Is that "just how they are," or can they change? God invites change. We can exchange foolishness for wisdom and ignorance for knowledge. But it comes at a price many choose not to pay. God insists on being God, and we must submit and yield to him.

In the California culture from which I write this, there is a beach subculture of young people who live for the sun and the surf. That is all fine until they turn forty-five or fifty and have weathered skin and no job or family. The simple way runs out over time. What will it take?

## "WHAT DO YOU MEAN BY CRUSHING MY PEOPLE AND GRINDING THE FACES OF THE POOR?"

*ISA. 3:15*

The last task the man was given on his last day of work in the manufacturing plant was to unbolt his machine from the floor so it could be lifted, packed, and sent overseas for someone to do his job at a cheaper rate of pay. He was crushed. His job was never going to return, and he was not alone. His whole cohort of friends was losing their jobs to the new globalized economy. Shareholders were happy and stock prices rose. But what about the workers? This story could be repeated in a variety of contexts—from single parents to returning veterans to retirees who lost their pensions to the chronically ill without sufficient insurance. Who cares? Who cares about the crushed ones around us? Whose responsibility are the faces of the poor in our midst?

But it's not my fault. I'm just a pastor (or insert your career title) doing my best. I didn't lay off anyone. The needs are too great for me. And those are all justified and accurate answers. But beneath this question is the question: what is my part in crushing people? What is my role in grinding the faces of the poor?

**"WHAT MORE COULD HAVE BEEN DONE FOR MY VINEYARD THAT I HAVE DONE FOR IT? WHEN I LOOKED FOR GOOD GRAPES, WHY DID IT YIELD ONLY BAD?"**

*ISA. 5:4*

I am really good at making excuses. I am a professional at justifying my conduct. I have a good reason for why things go the way that they do. Another chance; a little more time; lower the standard; look the other way.

God's question is penetrating. What more could he have done for Israel than he did? Begin with the Exodus and walk forward. Where was God miserly or cheap? Where was God harsh or unforgiving? Where did God refuse to give second, third, and fourth chances? Where did God not warn his people through prophets about the dangers of their behavior? *"What more?"* is a painful question to Israel and to me.

What more does God need to do in my life for me to get it, to be obedient, to be generous, to be forgiving, to be faithful? What more does God need to do in my life so that I can be loving and tender to my family and others? What more does God need to provide for me so that I can trust him and not fear? *What more?*

## "Who shall I send? And who will go for us?"

### *Isa. 6:8*

I don't like the word *volunteer* when it comes to church and faith. *Volunteering* seems so gracious on our part. We concede to *volunteering* our precious time and resources to this or that needy project so long as it measures up to our expectations. We *volunteer* to help so long as we have the extra time or energy (or money) to give to this or that organization.

This is the only text I can think of in the Bible, where God seems to be asking for a *volunteer*. God asks "Who?" and Isaiah says, "*Here am I, send me.*" Isaiah is a *volunteer*, or is he? Go back and read Isaiah 6:1-13 and ask, who else is in the audience? It's only Isaiah. Well, it's Isaiah and God (and some angels). And the question is, "*Who?*" Isaiah looks around the room for someone else, but nobody else is there. It's just him. As long as there are others in the audience who look younger, richer, more talented, and better able to help, I can keep my hand down. But when the question of *who* comes and I'm alone with God, what else can I say? Where are you hearing *who* today?

"**WHAT WILL YOU DO ON THE DAY OF RECKONING, WHEN DISASTER COMES FROM AFAR? TO WHOM WILL YOU RUN FOR HELP? WHERE WILL YOU LEAVE YOUR RICHES?**"

*ISA. 10:3*

It was a motley group. Six inner-city gang kids joined three of us youth workers for a canoeing adventure into Canada. It was pretty madcap at times—the ignorant leading the unwilling! One of the unanticipated experiences was a long portage, where you must carry your canoe overhead, surrounded by heavy clouds of mosquitoes. It was truly miserable! At one point, midway through a portage and three days into the wilderness, one boy threw down his canoe and said, "That's it! I quit! This is stupid!" (Though he used far more graphic terms).

It was a telling moment for us. So we asked him where he planned to go. What were his options? We were in the middle of nowhere. It was a time of reckoning for him and for us. He could not switch a channel or leave the area.

Many of us live like my young friend did. We think we are in control, sovereign and independent. We have our wealth stashed and our things around us. We have our routines and patterns, our traditions and customs. But when the *day of reckoning comes,* what will we do? And that day does come to all of us in the form of disaster, death, divorce, cancer, and change. Things change abruptly around us whether we give them permission or not. *What will you do?*

**"SHALL I NOT DEAL WITH JERUSALEM**

**AND HER IMAGES AS I DEALT WITH**

**SAMARIA AND HER IDOLS?"**

*ISA. 10:11*

There is a term used among sociologists and historians called *American Exceptionalism.* The concept asserts that America, as a nation, is exceptional in the world among all other nations. And without getting into a heated argument about this, we can admit that the United States has opportunities, advantages and strengths, which are unique among the nations of the world. But is exceptionalism a privilege or a responsibility?

Israel also considered itself exceptional for many reasons. They were chosen by God, given a covenant relationship and the promised land. God chose them among all the nations of the earth to both bless and enable them to bless others. But over time Israel saw its exceptionalism as all privilege and little responsibility. It saw its relationship with God as a "get out of jail free" card. Israel and God were fraternity buddies who could look the other way at indiscretions.

The question God asked Israel through Isaiah is about exceptionalism. Does God hold Israel to the same expectations as surrounding nations like Samaria? Will God punish the same sins the same way for different people? Is God fair or biased? Are my sins excusable because of who I am and how long I've been a Christian? Are my idols understandable and acceptable? Really?

**"DOES THE AX RAISE ITSELF ABOVE THE ONE WHO SWINGS IT, OR THE SAW BOAST AGAINST THE ONE WHO USES IT?"**

*ISA. 10:15*

We too soon forget. We forget what is ours from what is entrusted to us. We forget being stewards and too soon think of ourselves as owners. In the text above, God is going to punish the nation of Assyria for forgetting. They forgot that they were given power to served God's purposes and were now serving their own purposes. That's like the ax thinking that the cutter works for the ax or the saw as controlling the lumberman.

I do that all the time. I forget what has been entrusted to me for a while, for a brief period of time, and I soon think of these things as my own. Like what? My position as senior pastor of a church is not mine, but I can get used to the office, the title, and the salary, as well as my home, which is the parsonage of the church. Though I "know" it is owned by the church for me to live in as long as I'm the pastor, I like to think of it as "my house." I can even think of the church I serve as "my" church, especially when talking with other pastors.

List all those things you affix the label of "my" on today. What is yours and what has been given to you to use for God's purposes?

## "WHERE ARE YOUR WISE MEN NOW?"

### ISA. *19:12*

I'm impressed by wise people. I'm impressed by people who have earned PhD's and are called Dr. _____. When I am in a room full of academicians (which happens often in the church I serve, since it is next to a college), I am genuinely amazed by what they know and their grasp of information and facts.

I'm also impressed by wealthy people. I know it's just money, but I am amazed at how these creative persons turned initial investments into fortunes. I am impressed by people who built companies and invented products that we all know and use.

I'm also impressed by celebrities. In the community in which I now live, a number of celebrities also live. These are people the world knows by just their first name. They have faces that are famous. When they turn up at an event, cameras come out and crowds form. Their names and faces endorse products of all sorts, and, for that reason, we buy them. That amazes me!

But when the tough times come (as in the case of Egypt in the text above), where are the wise people? When the diagnosis is Alzheimer's or cancer, what friends or family show up? When your friends go through divorce or experience a loved one's death, where are the wise, the wealthy, and the celebrities? What and who carries us during the dark times?

"**WHAT TROUBLES YOU NOW THAT YOU HAVE
GONE UP TO YOUR ROOFS, YOU TOWN SO FULL OF
COMMOTION, YOU CITY OF TUMULT AND REVELRY?**"

*ISA. 22:1, 2*

The book of Isaiah is not a happy book. It's a book of judgment and endings. The nation of Israel is being punished for decades of faithlessness and spiritual compromises. God is calling the nation to account after generations of playing it light and easy with God's commands. From Isaiah 20 to this text, God announced that he is judging all the nations around Israel: Egypt, Cush, Babylon, Edom, Arabia, as well as Israel itself.

The question God asked above seeks to unmask a general sense of foreboding in Israel. Why go up to the roofs? What's on the roofs? A view, a vantage point, the horizon is visible from the roofs. The people have a gut sense that something is wrong—not enough to set down the tumult and revelry—but enough to go upstairs and take a look. Is anyone coming? Are there threats on the horizon?

Where are our roofs today? What do we *go up to* to see off in the distance or the future? The Dow Jones, investment portfolios, your pension fund balance, employment rates, or international relations? What are those indices that you look to for assurance or worry? What's going on in your *towns* around you?

"**WHAT ARE YOU DOING HERE AND WHO GAVE YOU
PERMISSION TO CUT OUT A GRAVE FOR YOURSELF
HERE, HEWING YOUR GRAVE ON THE HEIGHT AND
CHISELING YOUR RESTING PLACE IN THE ROCK?"**

*ISA. 22:16*

How do you think you will be remembered? What should be written on your gravestone? My father wanted, and was granted, the phrase "He was faithful" written on his plain gravestone in the Ft. Snelling Memorial Cemetery in Minneapolis.

What will be your legacy? In many cultures past and present, tombs and mausoleums are ways to imprint one's name on history. Large stone buildings with etched family names say "Important!" Leaving large amounts of money to institutions, guarantees family names affixed to buildings and even whole schools. Gifts to churches often come with the recognition plaque on a wall or fixture, "Given in memory of _____."

As a pastor, I have officiated hundreds of funeral services. In the planning portion with the family, a lot of energy is spent crafting and carefully wording the deceased person's life, often making him/her too good to be true: "Nicest guy in the world; she never said a bad thing about anyone; he'd give you the shirt off his back; she was too good for this world and God took her back to make her an angel!" Really? Who is in charge of your legacy?

"WHEN FARMERS PLOW FOR PLANTING, DO THEY PLOW
CONTINUALLY? DO THEY KEEP ON BREAKING UP AND WORKING
THE SOIL? WHEN THEY HAVE LEVELED THE SURFACE, DO THEY
NOT SOW CARAWAY AND SCATTER CUMIN?"

*ISA. 28:24, 25*

I'm neither a farmer nor a gardener. I appreciate grown foods and flowering plants, but I don't have the patience or commitment to the growing process. Gratefully, I'm married to a woman who loves the soil and all things growing. Martha has the wisdom to know when to work the soil and when to walk away and leave it. She has the farmer's rhythm of plowing and planting, of resting and waiting.

My problem is a lack of appreciation of the mystery of life and growth. I'm too much like a little child on a long trip, constantly asking, "Are we there yet?" I *plow* continually and have a hard time letting up. I can become a restless, spiritual nag, hounding people and beleaguering them with my impatience. I've done that with my children and church staff. I've done that with church leaders and whole congregations. Underneath this question is the underlying question of *when is it enough?* When have I done enough? When can I walk away and leave the mystery of growth to God?

> "SHALL WHAT IS FORMED SAY TO THE ONE WHO
> FORMED IT, 'YOU DID NOT MAKE ME?' CAN THE
> POT SAY TO THE POTTER 'YOU KNOW NOTHING?'"
>
> *ISA. 29:16*

My wife is an artist, a printmaker. In addition to being a gardener, she lives to make art. Every once in a while, when I am doing my chores of gathering and taking out the trash, I will empty her studio wastebasket and notice torn-up art! I'm shocked and disappointed. That was good art; why should she tear it up and throw it away? The answer is simple: she is the artist, not the paper nor I, the viewing public. The artist alone has the right (if not the mandate) to determine what is good and suitable and what is worthless.

The question above is wonderfully hyperbolic. It's almost sad humor to think of created objects claiming self-creation and judging their creator as stupid. Yet how many times do students evaluate their teachers as being ignorant? How many children consider their parents as worthless? How many of us read God's word regularly, yet think it is impractical and unrealistic for us today? Really?

## "HAVE YOU NOT HEARD?"

### ISA. 37:26

OK, I admit it. I have some hearing loss. I don't want to admit that I'm aging, but I do miss some words. And my wife has noticed that I often miss her words requesting me to do something! Hearing is important! When people come to church hungry to worship and can't hear the preacher that day, their response is acute and strong, often angry. We *want* to hear what we want to hear. But we do not always want to hear what we *need* to hear. We don't always want to hear words like *lose weight, less salt, more exercise, and cut out the doughnuts!*

The power of our relationship with God sits in this nexus of our hearing, of our reception of God's word to us, and our free responsibility to act on what we hear. God does not program us as spiritual robots, but gives us his word(s). The deep question is *have we not heard?* Is God asking us something totally new, or repeating something we have long been ignoring and have become "deaf" to? What is it that we are hearing from God today?

"WITH WHOM, THEN, WILL YOU COMPARE GOD?
TO WHAT IMAGE WILL YOU LIKEN HIM?"

*ISA. 40:18, 25*

What are the metaphors you employ for God? Is he grand designer, loving father, righteous judge, protector of our nation, distant creator, or intimate caregiver? As humans we tend to anthropomorphize God into recognizable images, concepts, and creations. We do that all the time. Yet, in this moment, God asked Israel and us to draw up a list of the words, concepts and images that we use for God (notice I did not use the masculine image of "him").

God demands uniqueness and being unchained from our images. God wants to break out of our cognitive cages and roam sovereign, alone as God. List your images and words, and let God be God.

"WHY DO YOU COMPLAIN JACOB? WHY DO YOU SAY,
ISRAEL, 'MY WAY IS HIDDEN FROM THE LORD; MY CAUSE
IS DISREGARDED BY MY GOD?' DO YOU NOT KNOW? HAVE
YOU NOT UNDERSTOOD? THE LORD IS THE EVERLASTING
GOD, THE CREATOR OF THE ENDS OF THE EARTH. HE WILL
NOT GROW TIRED OR WEARY."

*ISA. 40:28*

I have a friend who remembers everyone's birthdays. She is relentlessly making sure everyone knows about an upcoming birthday, passes around cards to be signed, and even bakes cakes for others' parties. Why? Well, growing up, her birthday was forgotten twice by her own mother! When she tells the story, as an adult now with her mother passed away for years, the pain still tinges her words.

Forgotten is a painful word. When someone forgets to call us, meet us, or do something for us that they promised to do, it hurts. It even makes us angry. Are we so unimportant that they forgot us?

But how about when it comes to God? How many of us, in honest moments, do feel forgotten by God? We have prayed the same prayers for the same people for years, and nothing has changed. We have prayed for healing, and the person died. We prayed for our children, and they walked away from the faith. We prayed for the nation, and the other party candidate became president. Did God forget? Where do you feel forgotten by God? The word after the question is assuring: *he will not grow tired or weary* like we do.

**"WHO IS BLIND BUT MY SERVANT, AND DEAF LIKE THE MESSENGER I SEND? WHO IS BLIND LIKE THE ONE IN COVENANT WITH ME, BLIND LIKE THE SERVANT OF THE LORD?"**

*ISA. 42:19*

I love seeing! I love looking out at the weather, no matter what it is. I love seeing the sun as it rises over the ocean or mist in a mountain valley. I love seeing nature in all its splendor and great art and delicious food. I love seeing sleek cars and elegant boats. Think of all the ways you delight in the world of sight. To be blind would be unimaginably difficult.

I have a friend who has lost his sight over the years. He was once sighted and is now functionally blind. He walks with an awkward gate of having fallen down, tripped, or stumbled too many times. His head twists to find recognizable voices. He doesn't always know where to reach or where the food is. He is of good spirit and makes the best of a tough situation. But blindness is not fun.

What does it mean when God calls his servant blind? What does it mean to be spiritually blind? Does blindness make us naïve or more vulnerable? Does blindness make us less usable by God and more susceptible to abuse and misleading? Ask God today to show you where you are blind, and ask him to heal you and make you see.

**"WHICH OF YOU WILL LISTEN TO THIS OR PAY**

**CLOSE ATTENTION IN TIME TO COME?"**

*ISA. 42:23*

At a restaurant recently, a family of four sat across from us in my line of sight. They were a healthy, good-looking family consisting of a mom, dad, adolescent son, and teenage daughter. Everything seemed fine with them except for one thing; the dad was continually pulling out his smart phone and texting on it. It was as if he regularly dropped out of the family's conversation and into whatever cyber activity claimed his attention. One thing was obvious; he was not paying attention to his children or wife as long as his phone was out.

How do you know you are paying attention—to another person or to God? What are your inner indicators that you are dialed into what God is doing? And, oppositely, how do you know you are not paying attention and are distracted? Ask God today to turn your attention to him, and see what happens.

**"WHICH OF THEIR GODS FORETOLD THIS AND PROCLAIMED TO US THE FORMER THINGS?"**

*ISA. 43:9*

Previously I said that Isaiah is not, generally, a fun book to read. It is full of tough things that God needed to say to Israel about their faithlessness and imminent judgment. They are going to lose their nation and their freedom. They would be invaded, sacked and taken into exile as slaves.

Although everything Isaiah said was painfully true, Isaiah 43 it says that the light shines brilliantly about what God promised to do for his punished and exiled people. He would bring them home, and he would sustain them in their exile with his love and power. This is the fundamental nature of God: love for his people even though they do not deserve it. He comes and loves them... and us.

What religion does this? What religion has a self-sacrificing and loving God who comes to us? This is not a slam on Islam, Buddhism, Hinduism or any other major world religions. But take a look and ask, which god comes in love for his children like Israel's God?

**"NO ONE CAN DELIVER OUT OF MY HAND. WHEN I**

**ACT, WHO CAN REVERSE IT?"**

*ISA. 43:13*

I don't accept judgments very well. I like knowing the reasoning and rationale behind a judgment. And if I don't agree, I like to appeal a decision. That's a fundamental value of western culture that is ruled by law. We have courts, appeals courts, state supreme courts, and the US Supreme Court. Most organizations have policies and procedures with appeals processes built in to insure fairness and good order. And we are used to appeals being granted and decisions reversed. People are found innocent after having served years on a wrongly convicted trial.

Do our litigious and appeal-driven values leak into our relationship with God? I know God accepts our asking *why* about things in life, but do we think we can argue our way out of God's actions? Where are you learning how to submit to God's actions? How's that going?

**"FORGET THE FORMER THINGS; DO NOT DWELL ON
THE PAST. SEE, I AM DOING A NEW THING! NOW IT
SPRINGS UP; DO YOU NOT PERCEIVE IT?"**

*ISA. 43:18, 19*

We forget the right things and remember the wrong things. I can easily forget God's promises and remember all the times others have slighted me. Years ago in Minnesota, I saw a young man with a four-digit number tattooed on his neck clearly visible for all to see. Since I did not think it was his home address, and it was too short for a phone number, I asked him about the significance of the number. He answered me severely saying that it was the date Muslims destroyed his family village! It was over 600 years ago! How's that for dwelling on the past?

But are we so different? Have we *tattooed* the names and infractions of others on our memories and refused to let them go? Do we remember the slights done to our children by other children or adults and still get angry? Do we continue to resent an injustice we experienced long ago and still carry blame?

The question behind this question is: will we allow God to do a new thing in our lives? God is doing new things; the question is—will we perceive it or miss it?

"I AM THE FIRST AND I AM THE LAST; APART FROM
ME THERE IS NOT GOD. WHO THEN IS LIKE ME?
IS THERE ANY GOD BESIDES ME? NO, THERE IS NO
OTHER ROCK; I KNOW NOT ONE."

*ISA. 44:6, 8*

I love menus, choices, and options in almost every area of life. I like choosing channels to watch or entrees to order. I like having wardrobe choices and shopping choices. I like having the freedom to choose fonts and layouts when I write. I like choosing travel destinations and activities. A recurring phrase in our culture is, "I don't like that one; I want a different one," and it can apply to anything.

The culture of choice affects the spiritual life as well. We shop for and choose churches, pastors, youth programs, and musical styles. We choose style, length of services, and programs to get involved in. And nothing is wrong with that...until it comes to God. Are we shopping for a different god when we do not like the word of God? Will we let God be God...alone?

"WHO SHAPES A GOD AND CASTS AN IDOL,
WHICH CAN PROFIT NOTHING?"

*ISA. 44:10*

I love motorcycles. In the past I have had four different motorcycles, the last one being the best, a Norton 650 cc Thunderbolt. My wife is used to me turning my head at the sound of a motorcycle and even identifying some by their sounds. A couple of years ago I saw the most beautiful motorcycle I had ever seen parked outside of a Starbucks. It was painted flat black and sculpted like a work of art. It was engineered in a way I had never seen. When the owner came out, I told him how much I admired the bike. He told me he had just purchased it and was breaking it in on a ride from Los Angeles to Santa Barbara for the day. I wanted that bike!

When I got home I looked up that bike on the Internet and discovered that the motorcycle sold for over $100,000! Immediately, I went from admiring this motorcycle to thinking it was the dumbest purchase anyone could ever make. It could fall over for goodness' sake. It was just a motorcycle! Who would spend that much money on a toy?

God asked Israel the same question. Idols are cool looking, well made, and often very impressive. But at the end of the day, they were made in shops by human hands and don't deliver what they promise.

What are the idols that slip into your life: clothing, your house or location, career, health, safety?

**"WHO FORETOLD THIS LONG AGO, WHO DECLARED IT FROM THE DISTANT PAST? WAS IT NOT I, THE LORD? AND THERE IS NO GOD APART FROM ME, A RIGHTEOUS SAVIOR; THERE IS NO ONE BUT ME."**

*ISA. 45:21*

Early in my faith life, I spent a year in Japan as a short-term missionary assisting the full-time missionaries in our denomination. One of my duties was to help teach English classes at a local outreach center. It required a long walk through neighborhoods and passing by an ancient Japanese cemetery. Each time I approached the cemetery my heart beat faster and my pace quickened. I imagined all the statues and images that were dedicated to a religion and god other than mine. I worried that there were evil spirits there that could grab and harm me. Each trip felt like a spiritual gauntlet that I had to endure and survive.

Then, on one day, God seemed to speak to me in a question: *what other gods threaten me?* In an instant I recognized that God alone was God. There were no other competing gods who could dislodge God. If God alone is God, as the quote and question above propose, who else is in spiritual competition? Who is in charge of the universe, history, time, and our destiny?

**"YOU HAVE HEARD THESE THINGS [INDICTMENTS];
LOOK AT THEM ALL. WILL YOU NOT ADMIT THEM?"**

*ISA. 48:6*

*I told you so* is not something our ears like to hear. We all like to be right in our own eyes and justify our behavior. We recast our histories with golden hues of innocence and righteousness. Our ancestors were noble and mighty, and we were more often the victims of other people's misdeeds than perpetrators.

In the verses (48:1-5) leading up to this question, God reminds Israel of its long history of rebelliousness and duplicity. Israel's character traits were stubbornness and spiritual inconsistency. Why are they so surprised? Why is it so hard for them (and us) to admit our long history of sinfulness?

**"HOW CAN I LET MYSELF BE DEFAMED? I WILL NOT YIELD MY GLORY TO ANOTHER."**

*ISA. 48:11*

Having the last word is something squabbling children push to the limit with the seesaw phrases: *Did so! Did not!* We hate being bested by another. We insist on saying just one more thing to clarify our case. But in this question today, God asks us if we really think he does not have the last word. Will God, in the end, allow us to critique him? Will God sit on the sidelines and let his cause be defamed forever? How can God's last word be of hope for you?

**"COME TOGETHER, ALL OF YOU, AND LISTEN:
WHICH OF THE IDOLS FORETOLD THESE THINGS?"**

*ISA. 48:14*

What amazes me throughout scripture is how vulnerable God is. God submits himself to our endless tests and scrutiny. God allows us to *test-drive* him in our lives and world to see if he really works, if he is really true and reliable. God's word accurately describes both history and the human condition. Which of our many idols does a better job than God?

"CAN A MOTHER FORGET THE BABY AT HER BREAST AND
HAVE NO COMPASSION ON THE CHILD SHE HAS BORNE?
THOUGH SHE MAY FORGET, I WILL NOT FORGET YOU!"
*ISA. 49:15*

I know a mother who lost her child at a young age. The circumstances surrounding her child's death called for an investigation and cast doubts on the care she and her husband provided. They were eventually cleared of all charges and declared innocent. It occurred over twenty years ago. But still, today, when she talks of her long-deceased child, her eyes well with tears, and her face flushes with pain. Mothers never forget (nor do fathers). Mothers, who first felt the twinge of life in their wombs and the traumatic moments of birth, do not forget their children. Mothers, who gaze endlessly down on faces puckered up with nursing motions, have their memories etched with their children.

Oh, children forget parents soon enough. In the desire for independence, children consider their parents as harsh jailors, unrealistic guards, and embarrassing old people. Children dream of leaving home and starting their own lives, routinely forgetting to call or write because they are so busy, but mothers (and fathers) do not forget their children—even when their children forget them.

However busy you are, however harried and frantic your world is today, God has not forgotten you.

### "CAN PLUNDER BE TAKEN FROM WARRIORS, OR CAPTIVES BE RESCUED FROM THE FIERCE?"

*ISA. 49:24*

The enemies are so great. The odds against us are enormous. What can we do? The situations around us are so big, many of us feel genuinely helpless to do much other than get through the day and survive. Our jobs, our finances, the culture around us seem overwhelming. So did Israel's situation appear to them in captivity, in a foreign country by a military superpower. Who can rescue us?

God answers the question he posed in verses 24 and 25 by saying that he will do the capturing and rescuing. As mighty as Israel's adversaries were, God is mightier then and now. Who captures you? What force intimidates you? Name it before God today.

"WHERE IS YOUR MOTHER'S CERTIFICATE OF DIVORCE WITH WHICH
I SENT HER AWAY? OR TO WHICH OF MY CREDITORS DID I SELL
YOU? BECAUSE OF YOUR SINS YOU WERE SOLD; BECAUSE OF YOUR
TRANSGRESSIONS YOUR MOTHER WAS SENT AWAY. WHEN I CAME,
WHY WAS THERE NO ONE? WHEN I CALLED, WHY WAS THERE NO
ONE TO ANSWER? WAS MY ARM TOO SHORT TO DELIVER YOU? DO I
LACK THE STRENGTH TO RESCUE YOU?"

*ISA. 50:1,2*

Who made this mess? Who is responsible for the way things are around us? Our culture loves to play the *blame game* all the time. The answer is usually someone else. Have you ever heard a newscaster, in asking a rhetorical question like this, pause, and say something like, "I think I'm the one to blame for some of this. The media industry to which I belong, traffics in the pain and suffering of others and we are part of the cause of it." I doubt you ever have or ever will hear such a response. I do the same thing all the time when I look at why something is not going well in the church I serve. I seldom say, "I think it's my fault. I'm just not as good a pastor as you need."

Yet, behind God's question is the three-letter answer: *sin*. Israel's life of intentional sin created the mess. But when God comes to heal and rescue, why is there no answer? Why does it seem like no one is home? Are you forgivable? Are you rescue-able? Is your life able to be fully redeemed and given another chance?

"WHO ARE YOU THAT FEAR MERE MORTALS, HUMAN BEINGS THAT
ARE BUT GRASS, THAT YOU FORGET THE LORD YOUR MAKER,
WHO STRETCHED OUT THE HEAVENS AND LAID THE FOUNDATIONS
OF THE EARTH, THAT YOU LIVE IN CONSTANT TERROR EVERY DAY
BECAUSE OF THE WRATH OF THE OPPRESSOR, WHO IS BENT ON
DESTRUCTION? FOR WHERE IS THE WRATH OF THE OPPRESSOR?"

*ISA. 51:12, 13*

I am amazed at my fear reflex. When I drive a car and am
following all the rules of the road, obeying speed limits and all
traffic signs, yet see a police-car, I am instantly nervous and alert.
I'm sure I've done something wrong, and my pulse quickens and
my heart races. In the few times I have been asked to serve on
jury duty, I get a dry throat when the judge asks me a question,
and I feel intimidated by the whole situation. I can get a fear
reflex visiting my doctor, dentist, or tax accountant. What's with
this? Why do I allow other people to trigger fear in me? Some
friends I know live in much greater fear of others all the time—
fear of not being accepted, being judged, or being criticized. They
worry and fret non-stop about what others think and say about
them. List the names of those people you fear today, and present
it as an offering to God. See what happens.

**"WHO HAS BELIEVED OUR MESSAGE AND TO WHOM HAS THE ARM OF THE LORD BEEN REVEALED?"**

*ISA. 53:1*

The rest of this passage is one of the most beautiful predictions and descriptions of the Messiah in the Old Testament. The Messiah, the savior of the entire world, is unlike any savior the world fashions. Everything about the Messiah is counterintuitive to a rescuer: insignificant, despised, rejected, sufferer, low-esteemed, stricken, crushed, and wounded. Who believes a Messiah like this one?

We are tempted at times to make Jesus the Messiah a bit more believable, a bit stronger, more robust and tough. Who believes in this message today?

**"WHY DO YOU SPEND YOUR MONEY ON WHAT IS NOT BREAD, AND YOUR LABOR ON WHAT DOES NOT SATISFY?"**

*ISA. 55:2*

What makes me crazy is seeing poor people buying lottery tickets. I see it all the time in convenience stores. Men and women, who are poorly clothed and should spend their money wisely, opt for a fantasy gamble of making it rich by choosing random numbers. I watch them furtively scratch their tickets, hoping for something good, and then I see the downcast eyes as they go bust again.

But it's like that in every sector of society; people are spiritually and physically hungry but spend their money and energy on junk. Why is that? What's the draw? Where do you get sucked in to spending on that which does not satisfy?

**"WHOM ARE YOU MOCKING? AT WHOM DO YOU SNEER AND STICK OUT YOUR TONGUE? ARE YOU NOT A BROOD OF REBELS, THE OFFSPRING OF LIARS?"**

*ISA. 57:4*

These three verbs are pretty volatile for us: *mock, sneer, stick out your tongue*. What's God asking here? Is he asking about a type of behavior known by sneering, mocking, and rude ridicule? Do you ever find yourself caught up in mocking a political leader you disagree with or sneering at an idea you object to? Have you gone so far as to stick out your tongue, or raise your fist, or physically show your disdain for a person? What does God think about that behavior?

## "IN VIEW OF ALL THIS, SHOULD I RELENT?"

### *ISA. 57:6*

The NPR radio show "A Prairie Home Companion" has a phrase created by founder Garrison Keillor describing the mythical town of Lake Wobegon, "All the men are good looking, the women are strong and all the children are above average." Is that possible? In much of current western culture every child is exceptional, every piece of art or music is a masterpiece, and no child can ever fail. Really? Does everyone have to win? What about bad behavior? What about substandard performance? What about violation of the rules? Does God have to relent and let everyone get by?

"WHOM HAVE YOU SO DREADED AND FEARED THAT YOU HAVE NOT BEEN TRUE TO ME, AND NEITHER REMEMBERED ME NOR TAKEN THIS TO HEART? IS IT NOT THAT I HAVE BEEN LONG SILENT THAT YOU DO NOT FEAR ME? IS IT NOT BECAUSE I HAVE LONG BEEN SILENT THAT YOU DO NOT FEAR ME?"

*ISA. 57:11, 12*

What keeps you from God? What prevents you from living a life in full obedience to God? What gets in your way from discipleship? God's question points us to whom and what we fear. Does the fear of failure keep you from God? Does the fear of acceptance keep you silent? Does the pressure to go along with your peer group keep you from being true to God? Who are the spiritual bullies in your life that foster spiritual fear?

"IS THIS THE KIND OF FAST I HAVE CHOSEN, ONLY
A DAY FOR PEOPLE TO HUMBLE THEMSELVES? IS IT
ONLY FOR BOWING ONE'S HEAD LIKE A REED AND FOR
LYING IN SACKCLOTH AND ASHES? IS THAT WHAT YOU
CALL A FAST, A DAY ACCEPTABLE TO THE LORD?"

*ISA. 58:5*

You do not have to read very far into the Bible to realize how unimpressed God is with religion. Religion as the human institutions and organizations that attach themselves to God seem to be layered in complexity. We love the elaborate and the spectacular. We love going to pageants and concerts with great fanfare and pomp. We love parades and processions, filled with dignitaries and elaborate rituals.

What impresses God? What gets God's attention?

**"IS IT NOT TO SHARE YOUR FOOD WITH THE HUNGRY AND TO PROVIDE THE POOR WANDERER WITH SHELTER—WHEN YOU SEE THE NAKED TO CLOTHE THEM, AND NOT TURN AWAY FROM YOUR OWN FLESH AND BLOOD?"**

*ISA. 58:7*

God is less impressed with what goes on inside a church on a Sunday morning than what happens through that church to the homeless person who knocks on the door on Tuesday afternoon. Where does your faith speak to justice, compassion, and mercy? Where has sharing fit into your discipleship?

**"WHERE IS THE HOUSE YOU WILL BUILD FOR ME? WHERE WILL MY RESTING PLACE BE? HAS NOT MY HAND MADE ALL THESE THINGS, AND SO THEY CAME INTO BEING?"**

*ISA. 66:1, 2*

I like our house. I like the way our house is furnished and outfitted just for our tastes. I have my chairs and spaces and Martha has hers. I have acceded to her need for dainty and elegant, and she has conceded to my need for larger and comfortable. Over time every family makes their house their own. Think about some of the ways you love your house.

The question beneath this question today is: do we make God's house for God or for us? How does the church you regularly worship in reflect God's tastes, and how does it reflect the tastes of the community and denomination? How can God break out of the houses we make for him into all of creation?

"'WHO HAS EVER HEARD OF SUCH THINGS? WHO HAS EVER SEEN THINGS LIKE THIS? CAN A COUNTRY BE BORN IN A DAY OR A NATION BE BROUGHT FORTH IN A MOMENT? DO I BRING TO THE MOMENT OF BIRTH AND NOT DELIVER?' SAYS THE LORD. 'DO I CLOSE UP THE WOMB WHEN I BRING TO DELIVERY?' SAYS YOUR GOD."

*ISA. 66:8, 9*

As a man, I am uniquely unqualified to talk about labor and delivery. However, as a husband, father, and grandfather I have observed my share (3 children and 1 grandchild) of pregnancies, labors, and deliveries. They are nothing short of monumental, intense, grueling, frightening, painful, exhausting, and joyful. It's a long process for the mother from conception through all the distortions pregnancy creates in her body to the cataclysmic release of the baby into the world of air and light. It does not *just happen*. That process can beautifully strengthen marriages, as fathers and mothers learn to lean on and trust each other through long months and critical hours.

God positions himself in this question like a midwife or obstetrician. He is patient in walking us through out spiritual *birthing*. It does not just happen; rather, it takes time and patience. Identify some *birthing stages* in your spiritual life today and thank God for his presence.

## "WHAT DO YOU SEE?"

### JER. *1:11, 13*

I identify with Jeremiah's reluctance. He did not want to become a prophet and even fought against it. But God called (maybe dragged) Jeremiah into his service. Throughout the book of Jeremiah God's word *comes* to Jeremiah. It's as if he is standing around, minding his own business, and God's word slams into him like a truck.

One of the first questions God's word asked Jeremiah was the question above: *what do you see?* That question needs a follow-up question: *where are you looking* or *what are you looking at?*

Living with an artist has taught me a lot about seeing. Martha sees things completely differently than I do. She sees colors and lines and patterns, when all I see is a barn and a field. She has taught me to see the world around us as a canvas full of surprises, delights, and jokes. But as a pastor, I have learned over the years to *see* people differently. I see people as who they long to be or who they grieve they will never become. I see people still carrying the wounds of childhood wrapped in the trappings of power. I see a great deal of pain underneath the makeup of success and beauty. What do you see?

"WHAT FAULT DID YOUR ANCESTORS FIND IN ME,
THAT THEY STRAYED SO FAR FROM ME?"

*JER. 2:4*

As I meet with couples preparing to get married, I have begun asking them about their spiritual autobiographies beginning with their grandparents. This is a fascinating conversation. I ask them what they learned about God by observing their grandparents' behavior or lifestyles. Many couples stare at me blankly, not knowing what to say. Some never observed their grandparents; others pause and dig deeply into routines and customs that spoke or did not speak about God. It's a time of genuine discovery, and more than one couple has gone back to their parents for more information. The next question I ask is about their own parents, their family of origin. What did they learn from mom and dad?

We are not self-invented. We have stories, precedents, and origins. It matters what our families did and did not do. What do you know about what happened to your ancestors and why they were where they were spiritually?

**"Has a nation ever changed its gods? (Yet they are not gods at all.)"**

*Jer. 2:11*

I am not a big football fan, but my father was. Growing up in Northern Michigan, football for him was a moral contest between forces of good and evil, dark and light. He brought complicated moral scenarios to every game and there were clearly valiant teams that deserved to win and evil teams that needed to be vanquished. Watching football games with my dad was intense!

Nothing disgusted him more than when a team left a city and was purchased by some millionaire in another region of the country. He felt betrayed by the team and never rooted for it again, and he felt sad for the city abandoned by its sports team. How about gods? Who abandons God? Who abandons gods? What's the difference?

**"HOW THEN DID YOU TURN AGAINST ME INTO A CORRUPT, WILD VINE?"**

*JER. 2:21*

We were such naïve parents. We were studiously careful to provide the same treatment to each of our three children: toys, food, nurture, one-on-one time, etc. They all came from the same womb, nursed from the same breast, were fed the same foods. Yet each one is so very different from the others! Each one responded to their environment differently from their siblings.

God is asking a bewildering question not unlike that of parents. What happened? What caused you to turn away? What made you go wild? Look at your paths, the times you turned away from God. How did that happen?

**"WHERE ARE THE GODS YOU MADE FOR YOURSELF?
LET THEM COME IF THEY CAN SAVE YOU WHEN YOU
ARE IN TROUBLE."**

*JER. 2:28*

Jesus said, "Where your treasure is, there will your heart be also." (Matt. 6:21) meaning that our hearts value (dare I say worship?) those things/persons we consider to be our greatest treasures. We value what we worship, and we worship what we value. Idolatry is not so overt as bowing down before carved statues. Idolatry is what captures our time, energy, and imagination. Idols are what keep us up at night and quicken our pulse. Idols are what we allow to interrupt us and send us off on a tangent.

When the storm clouds pile up and the foundations of life tremble, how good are those idols, those gods, those passions?

"HAVE I BEEN A DESERT TO ISRAEL OR A LAND OF GREAT DARKNESS? WHY DO MY PEOPLE SAY, 'WE ARE FREE TO ROAM; WE WILL COME TO YOU NO MORE?'"

*JER. 2:31*

While skiing in Austria many years ago, I saw a sign warning of a dangerous crevasse. I asked my Austrian friend who worked for the ski area if many people died there? "Oh yes," he said, "primarily Swedes and Americans." When I asked why Swedes and Americans, he said, "The Swedes come here to drink and party and don't see the signs. The Americans see the signs, cross over them asking 'Where is the crevasse?' and fall in!"

The people of Israel forgot that the desert was a place of danger and that the pillar of light was a gift in the darkness. They ignored God's boundaries and turned their spiritual desert into a playground where they thought they could freely wander without danger. Where are the boundaries you ignore? Where do you roam from God?

**"DOES A YOUNG WOMAN FORGET HER JEWELRY, A BRIDE HER WEDDING ORNAMENTS?"**

*JER. 2:32*

I've learned that my wife loves it when I buy her jewelry. I know what stones and metals she likes. I don't buy clothing or furniture, but jewelry works. And after more than thirty years of marriage, she has amassed a good number of necklaces, pendants, and earrings. What's amazing to me is that when I ask, "Where did you get that _____?" She responds instantly with the date, location, reason, and who gave it to her. She *knows* her jewelry! I would be shocked if she would answer, "I don't know where that necklace came from"!

How does a person forget something precious and important? God is both bewildered and pained that Israel regularly forgets their relationship to him. What goes on in our lives to make us forget God?

## "WHY DO YOU GO ABOUT SO MUCH, CHANGING YOUR WAYS?"

### JER. 2:36

Confirmation class is one of my deepest delights. My wife and I have been teaching Confirmation together for many years now. What is so fun is to see the way these young people change before our eyes. 7th and 8th graders (12-14 years old) often morph from little girls and boys into young women and young men. They vacillate between silliness and maturity, sometimes over the space of 20 minutes! That's what adolescence is all about, discovering who you are going to be, and we are privileged to be a part of that maturing process.

Israel was not an adolescent. Israel was a mature nation (or so it should have been), yet it kept vacillating between religions, traditions, and loyalties. It could not make up its mind whom it would serve. They simply switched between other nations and other gods. Where have you been changing, and where are you remaining committed? Where would you like to stop changing your ways?

## "BUT YOU HAVE LIVED AS A PROSTITUTE WITH MANY LOVERS—WOULD YOU NOW RETURN TO ME?"

*JER. 3:1*

This is a question for mature audiences only. There are times and places in the Bible where I almost shudder at the graphic nature of the language. This is not a question for young children or innocent audiences. Prostitution remains an ugly reality even today. It is called by many names: the sex trade, adult entertainment, escort services, human trafficking, sexual abuse, sexual addiction. It is neither innocent nor simple. It demeans what God intended as sacred and special. It makes crude what is meant to be tender. It sells what is meant to be given. It makes ugly what is meant to be beautiful. It devalues what is meant to be precious. There is no worse name a husband could call his wife than to call her a *prostitute*. And that's what God called Israel! How can a prostitute return to her husband after years of selling her body? How does God see us?

"LOOK UP TO THE BARREN HEIGHTS AND SEE. IS THERE
ANY PLACE WHERE YOU HAVE NOT BEEN RAVISHED?"

*JER. 3:2*

This is a negative question. When we confess our sins to
God, we often list specific sins, times, persons, and places where
we know we sinned. Here God asks a more blunt and brutal
question: "Where did you *not* sin?" Are there any places out of
bounds for our sinning?

## "HOW LONG WILL YOU HARBOR WICKED THOUGHTS?"

### JER. 4:14

As a little child I thought I could fool my mother. I would steal a cookie from the cookie jar or plate and stuff it into my mouth. If my lips were closed, I thought she couldn't see what I had in my mouth. I was always so surprised when she would say, "Don, are you eating a cookie?" "How did she know?" I wondered with bulging cheeks.

How does God know the junk we *harbor* in our minds? *Harbor* is an interesting word; it means a place safe and secure, out of the way of winds and storms, where a boat can rest securely. How do we *give harbor* to wicked thoughts? How do we keep them *protected* from the scrutiny of others or of God's Word? Ask God to show you *harbored thoughts* in your heart and mind today.

**"WHAT ARE YOU DOING, YOU DEVASTATED ONE? WHY DRESS YOURSELF IN SCARLET AND PUT ON JEWELS OF GOLD? WHY COLOR YOUR EYES WITH PAINT?"**

*JER. 4:30*

You know the conversations we have at church or at parties: "How's it going? Oh great! Just fantastic!" we lie. We dress up, put on makeup, wear nice cologne, and slap a happy smile on our faces. We pretend all is well, when it isn't. We can't let anyone know our lives are in shambles, and we are desperately pretending to have it together. We have such a hard time being honest with each other and with God. We spend our lives going and going and going...where? And note how God addressed Israel as *devastated one*. Is that judgmental or incredibly tender?

**"WHY SHOULD I FORGIVE YOU? YOUR
CHILDREN HAVE FORSAKEN ME AND SWORN BY
GODS THAT ARE NOT GODS."**

*JER. 5:7*

Can there be forgiveness without repentance? Can we expect God to forgive us if we do not intend to change our ways or forsake our sins? Israel wants cheap and easy forgiveness, while continuing in ways that take her away from God. Really? Why should God forgive Israel? Why should God forgive you?

**"'SHOULD I NOT PUNISH THEM FOR THIS?'
DECLARES THE LORD. 'SHOULD I NOT AVENGE
MYSELF ON SUCH A NATION AS THIS?'"**
*JER 5:9, 29, 9:10*

It's as if the judge invited us into his/her chamber to pour over the evidence and the decision of the jury. The sentencing phase of the trial is now underway and he/she wants us to examine all the evidence together. What should the judge do? Is punishment warranted after all the facts have been compiled? What do you think God should do to Israel? What do you think God should do to you?

**"'SHOULD YOU NOT FEAR ME?' DECLARES THE LORD.**
**'SHOULD YOU NOT TREMBLE IN MY PRESENCE?'"**
*JER 5:22*

I like the informality I experience on the West Coast. Whereas I used to wear ties every day in the Midwest, I now only wear ties on Sundays. I enjoy casual clothing and the more relaxed atmosphere of the California lifestyle. People in our community are not addressed by titles like "Dr.," "president," or even "Mr." or "Mrs." Instead, first names are used everywhere. I have experienced a name morph at the local barbershop from "Pastor Don" to "Pastor D" to "DJ" to "P-Diddly"! I'm not sure I like it. I know there is affection in it, but it is also kind of silly and demeaning. I'm not a 20-year-old hip-hop artist.

How do we know if we've become too casual with God? Where does intimacy and familiarity deteriorate into disrespect and disregard? Where does healthy spiritual fear fit into your relationship with God?

## "ARE THEY NOT ASHAMED OF THEIR DETESTABLE CONDUCT?"

### JER. 6:15

This is a question addressed to prophets, priests, and religious leaders. In verses 13 and 14 God, accused them of malpractice, of being greedy for gain, and of not taking care of the real needs of people. God accused them of lightly bandaging serious wounds.

I wonder sometimes if God asks that question of us pastors and leaders who run church programs and services. We try to put on a good program within an hour, keep people entertained and happy, and get them out of the door by noon. All the while, they are dying from fatal wounds. What would happen if we really went from being managers of programs, budgets, and buildings to really caring for the wounded? What would church look like? What would you and I look like?

> **"WHAT DO I CARE ABOUT INCENSE FROM SHEBA**
> **OR SWEET CALAMUS FROM A DISTANT LAND? YOUR**
> **BURNT OFFERINGS ARE NOT ACCEPTABLE; YOUR**
> **SACRIFICES DO NOT PLEASE ME."**
>
> *JER. 6:20*

If we leave people alone for too long with a project, it will get complicated. The same thing is true with committees. Too many people and too much time create inordinate levels of complexity. We can argue about font size and paper stock, background video and candle diameters. We can invest a great deal of time into types of coffee to serve (a fairly big deal for me) or punctuation accuracy in the bulletin (not a big deal to me but to others).

The question is: *what does God care?* That we do not know what incense from Sheba smells like, or even what sweet calamus is, drives the point home even further. How do we know what God really cares about? What if our greatest concerns are not what God cares about? What then?

**"Do you not see what they are doing in the towns of Judah and in the streets of Jerusalem?"**
*Jer. 7: 17*

I heard a statistic several years ago that I did not want to know. The Mall of America, in Bloomington, Minnesota, where I used to live, is the single largest location for human trafficking of minors for sex trade in the Midwest. The numbers were alarming at how many young people were drawn into or kidnapped for sex trafficking and how many meetings were arranged out of the Mall of America, that bastion of wholesome consumerism. I never saw it, but now I know. The question is: what will we do?

Do you and I know what's going on in the towns and streets where we live? Do we see? Do we care? What does it matter?

> **"'But am I the one they are provoking?'**
> **declares the Lord. 'Are they not rather**
> **harming themselves, to their own shame?'"**
> *Jer. 7:19*

Have you ever heard a child say in anger, "I'll just hold my breath 'till I die!" trying to blackmail a parent into doing what she/he wants them to do? Wise parents will react calmly and allow the child to go ahead and hold their breath until they either release and gasp for air or pass out and gasp for air. They will not die but only hurt (or embarrass) themselves.

Who is it that gets damaged by sin—God or us? Where could you be harming yourself today—physically, emotionally or spiritually? Are you willing to let God show you?

**"WHEN PEOPLE FALL DOWN, DO THEY NOT GET UP?**

**WHEN PEOPLE TURN AWAY, DO THEY NOT RETURN?**

**WHY THEN HAVE THESE PEOPLE TURNED AWAY?**

**WHY DOES JERUSALEM ALWAYS TURN AWAY?"**

*JER. 8:4, 5*

When I was learning to sail little Sunfish sailboats, a more experienced sailor gave me great advice: *when you get in trouble and are about to tip over, just let go of everything, and the boat will right itself and point into the wind.* He was right. Sailboats naturally right themselves and calm themselves. Humans have some instinctual responses as well. We flinch; we secrete adrenaline; we blink; we thrust out our hands to break a fall; we stand back up when we fall down. We are made to survive and thrive.

God made us to know him (Romans 1:19, 20). We are made to want God, to turn toward God, to trust in God. How come we keep turning away?

"HOW CAN YOU SAY 'WE ARE WISE, FOR WE HAVE
THE LAW OF THE LORD,' WHEN ACTUALLY THE LYING
PEN OF THE SCRIBES HAVE HANDLED IT FALSELY?"
*JER. 8:8*

I recently read about a man who received an award for his role in managing awards shows. The award show industry has competition among itself and awards itself awards for awards in no other place than Las Vegas! True story! How can they do that? But we do that all the time to ourselves; we fool ourselves in our superiority. I also read about the inherent problem in the American myth of the *World Series* in baseball. How can it be a *world* series with no other countries participating? Where are the baseball teams from Asia and South and Central America?

How can we call ourselves wise because we have what is called a "terminal degree"? Does a PhD make a person wise in all things? Where do you need to re-evaluate your own perception of wisdom?

**"ARE THEY ASHAMED OF THEIR DETESTABLE**

**CONDUCT? NO, THEY HAVE NO SHAME AT ALL."**

*JER. 8:12*

When was the last time you were personally ashamed? What caused your shame? For many in our culture, we avoid shame at all costs. In fact, we resent shame and think it is both unhealthy and inappropriate. Shame belongs, we think, to the culture of domination and the abuse of power. Shame is properly the precursor to confession of sin. Sin is not a mistake or an illness; it is shameful. It's something I should not have done. It's something about which I feel badly. What is your shame sensor like today?

**"WHY HAVE THEY AROUSED MY ANGER WITH THEIR IMAGES, WITH THEIR WORTHLESS FOREIGN IDOLS?"**

*JER. 8:19*

Swastikas arouse anger. Torture arouses anger. The sexual abuse of children arouses anger. Corporate greed and dishonesty arouse anger. Bullies arouse our anger. We know when our anger is aroused. It can happen in a minute—when a person cuts us off in their vehicle or gives us an angry hand signal.

Do you know what arouses God's anger?

**"Is there no balm in Gilead? Is there no physician there? Why then is there no healing for my people?"**

*Jer. 8:22*

My mother's cousin was a medical missionary in the Democratic Republic of Congo. I had the chance to see him perform surgery when we visited Congo many years ago. The conditions were abhorrent! There was no sterilized operating room (screens on the windows and curtains as doors); there were very few drugs but overwhelming needs. Fifty percent of his surgical patients died! "How do you do it?" I asked. He calmly said that if he were not there, a hundred percent would die. That's a real doctor!

Why is there no healing for God's people—physically, emotionally, and spiritually today? Does God lack resources to heal? Has God not given talents to his people to bring healing to all kinds of broken places? As you read and reflect on this question today, where is God asking you to bring healing to someone else?

**"SEE, I WILL REFINE THEM AND TEST THEM, FOR WHAT ELSE CAN I DO BECAUSE OF THE SIN OF MY PEOPLE?"**

*JER. 9:7*

We like to visit a little village in southern France called Biot. Biot is known for its excellent glassworks. All over the village are glassblowers with their furnaces and equipment. Showrooms have windows or viewing areas to watch the glassblowers in operation. When a piece of work is not going as planned, if it warps or has a flaw, it goes right back into the furnace to be refined and purified. It's the only way to get the glass pure.

How has God refined, purified, and fired your life? Where have you sensed God searing out the sin in your life with his righteous fire?

**"IF YOU HAVE RACED WITH PEOPLE ON FOOT AND THEY HAVE WORN YOU OUT, HOW CAN YOU COMPETE WITH HORSES? IF YOU STUMBLE IN SAFE COUNTRY, HOW WILL YOU MANAGE IN THE THICKETS BY THE JORDAN?"**

*JER. 12:5*

I have such low standards. I look at my pastoral life in the United States and complain about the stress of secularity and the distractions of prosperity. I stress about committee meeting conflicts and budget allocations. I worry about song choices and the cleanliness of the sanctuary. I get caught up in discussions about whether our church vehicles need replacement. And I go to bed exhausted.

Then I met three pastors—two from Cairo and one from Kenya. The pastor from Kenya belonged to the wrong tribe after an election and had his church, the orphanage he ran, and his home burned to the ground. He barely escaped with his life! But when fires came through California, he and his church prayed for us! My other two pastoral friends, who serve in Cairo, are routinely threatened with violence and arrest; yet, they praise God for his faithfulness and the converts they see coming to faith. Who's running with the horses?

**"Has not my inheritance become to me like a speckled bird of prey that other birds of prey surround and attack?"**

*Jer. 12:9*

Do you know any people who behave like targets? These are people who set themselves up for conflict and attack. These are people who knowingly provoke others. These are people who will wear clothing with outrageous comments or images, designed to trigger a reaction. There is a slight difference between young people who are experimenting with identity and lifestyle and those who set themselves up as targets. Another term for target is *bird of prey*, meaning that they will be eaten. These targets, God says in pain, are his inheritance, and they are heading for self-destruction.

Who in your circle has great spiritual potential, yet is behaving like a target? Pray for them by name today.

**"WHO WILL HAVE PITY ON YOU, JERUSALEM? WHO
WILL MOURN FOR YOU? WHO WILL STOP TO ASK
HOW YOU ARE?"**

*JER. 15:5*

He's a really bright guy. He is a talented photographer and musician. He's got a quick wit, and he cares for other people. But he's an addict. He does not stop getting drunk or high. He's been kicked out of schools and jobs, been arrested, wrecked his vehicles, and lost his home. He is caught in a web of addiction and bad choices. As much as I love him, I no longer ask him how he is. I know...he's drunk.

The verses that follow our question for today give a long and painful list of Israel's "addictions": rejection, backsliding, rebellion, stubbornness. Who will stop and ask *how you are*? I might have given up on this guy I describe above, but has God? How far does grace extend?

**"THE HEART IS DECEITFUL ABOVE ALL THINGS AND BEYOND CURE. WHO CAN UNDERSTAND IT?"**

*JER. 17:9*

It's a bleak statement, but is it true? How deeply deceitful is the human heart? Why do people keep lying when all the evidence convicts them? How is it that we justify a bad habit, even though we know it will hurt us? Why do we say words that we know will hurt someone, even though we profess that we love that person? Is the point of this question actually understanding the workings of the human heart, or confessing it?

"CAN I NOT DO WITH YOU, HOUSE OF ISRAEL, AS
THIS POTTER DOES?"

*JER. 18:6*

Potters and artists of all types routinely reject their work as inferior and start over. A good artist has standards far higher than his/her audience does. When people greet me at the door of church after I have preached a mediocre sermon and thank me for the good message, I'm not fooled. I could have done better.

This question asks the underlying question of who works for whom? Does God exist for Israel's satisfaction and blessing, or does Israel exist for God? Does God work for the advancement of your church, or do we exist for God and his pleasure? Can he do with us as he will?

"WHO HAS EVER HEARD ANYTHING LIKE THIS?
DOES THE SNOW OF LEBANON EVER VANISH FROM
ITS ROCKY SLOPES? DO COOL WATERS FROM
DISTANT SOURCES EVER CEASE TO FLOW? YET MY
PEOPLE HAVE FORGOTTEN ME."

*JER. 18:13-15*

Obviously, this question was not formed in the presence of global warming and the retreat of icebergs and glaciers. But in the presence of current scientific studies, we recoil in horror at what this means. If the snow melts, never to return, and the cool mountain waters cease to flow, what happens then? Everything changes in ways we are just beginning to experience.

Global warming is to science what forgetting is to faith. When people of faith forget God (choose to forget him), major things happen, and none of them are good. Where do you see forgetfulness in your community or circle of faith?

"DOES IT MAKE YOU A KING TO HAVE MORE AND
MORE CEDAR? DID NOT YOUR FATHER HAVE FOOD
AND DRINK? HE DID WHAT WAS RIGHT AND JUST, SO
ALL WENT WELL WITH HIM. HE DEFENDED THE CAUSE
OF THE POOR AND NEEDY, SO ALL WENT WELL. IS
THAT NOT WHAT IT MEANT TO KNOW ME?"

*JER. 22:15, 16*

How much stuff makes a person wealthy? According to
legend, John D. Rockefeller said, "Just a little bit more." The
desire to be "king of our own castle" is both a prevalent and
dangerous preoccupation. We build bigger, buy more, and pursue
nicer things in an attempt at self-sufficiency and independence
(the image of royalty). That's too European and not biblical
enough. According to the Old Testament, kings were anointed
in a covenantal ceremony, where God imposed obligations on
the king to do justice, to care for the poor and the foreigner.
How does that stack up to our vision of personal royalty?

## "WHY WILL HE AND HIS CHILDREN BE HURLED OUT, CAST INTO A LAND THEY DO NOT KNOW?"

### *JER. 22:28*

There is a long and complicated back-story to the failed leadership of King Jehoiachin in Jer. 22:18-28. He chose a rebellious and selfish path for his kingship, and the cost was passed on to his children. They would be exiled. I think of the recent kingdom collapses of despotic reigns of Muhmar Khadaffi in Libya, Sadam Hussein in Iraq, Hosni Mubarrak in Egypt, and Hafez Assad currently (as this is written) in Syria. Who paid the price? Their children and families did, often in cruel and horrible ways.

What blinds people to the long-term consequences of sinfulness? Is it so hard to obey and submit to God if it means good for one's family and community?

**"BUT WHICH OF THEM HAS STOOD IN THE COUNCIL**
**OF THE LORD TO SEE OR TO HEAR HIS WORD?**
**WHO HAS LISTENED AND HEARD HIS WORD?"**
*JER. 23:18*

How many news shows are little more than pooled ignorance and oversized egos? When breaking events happen, many news organizations pull in their "experts" to analyze what we know so far and to extrapolate on what could be happening; weather, war, politics, sports and the economy are all playgrounds for this. But who really knows? Primary players usually know, and they do not talk with the media.

Jeremiah is told by God to warn the people of Israel to stop listening to all the professional, religious types, who spout and spin theories and predictions based on their self-aggrandizement of power and influence. The question believers should ask about their pastors and leaders are the two above: *who has stood in the council of the Lord? Who has listened and heard his word?* Whose word have you heard and listened to

> **"'AM I ONLY A GOD NEARBY,' DECLARES THE LORD, 'AND NOT A GOD FAR AWAY? WHO CAN HIDE IN SECRET PLACES SO THAT I CANNOT SEE THEM?' DECLARES THE LORD. 'DO I NOT FILL HEAVEN AND EARTH?' DECLARES THE LORD."**
>
> *JER. 23:23, 24*

For many people, faith is defined by localism. They worship God in their local church with their local people in their well-known and comfortable ways. God is neatly confined and defined by their faith community in their own unique, theological box. God is practical and accessible. God helps them with jobs, marriages, health, and personal finance. God is up close and intimate and very responsive to our every need and request. And in many ways all this is true.

God is also distant and foreign. I know this first-hand, after worshiping with believers in Kenya, Congo, Egypt, France, and Greece. Their words are different. Their worship style is different. Their architecture is different. Their organizational structure is different. And they still are part of God's family, the church. Where is God far off for you in good and mysterious ways?

**"HOW LONG WILL THIS CONTINUE IN THE HEARTS OF THESE LYING PROPHETS, WHO PROPHESY THE DELUSIONS OF THEIR OWN MINDS?"**

*JER. 23:26*

There is enormous pressure on American pastors (all the ones I know) to be leaders who cast compelling visions. I am often asked by prospective members, "So, what's your vision for this church?" And I try to convey an exciting picture of what I believe God wants to do in this community in and through the church I serve. But seldom do I say something like: "God's vision for this church is to prune it of unfaithfulness and wean it from consumer passivity." I try to convey (or is the word *sell* more honest?) something positive and winsome, something that will make others want to belong to the church I serve.

Am I *prophesying* a *delusion of my own mind?* How do you know a prophecy could be a delusion of your own mind? When we always win and come out on top. When we pay little and others pay more. When we are right and others are wrong. Where could delusion fit into your own personal theology?

"'IS NOT MY WORD LIKE FIRE,' DECLARES THE LORD,

'AND LIKE A HAMMER THAT BREAKS A ROCK IN PIECES?'"

*JER. 23:29*

What are your favorite metaphors for God's Word in your life: food, water, light, life, hope, mercy, still waters that restore your soul, deep streams of water, a rich banquet feast? What would you add? I lean toward comfort. I like wrapping myself up in grace and love, mercy and hope. I like to underline words of assurance and forgiveness. I like to make God's word a warm comforter wrapped around me on a cold night.

Is that all? Where does God's word act as fire and hammer? When did God's word last scorch you or break you?

"ASK AND SEE: CAN A MAN BEAR CHILDREN? THEN
WHY DO I SEE EVERY STRONG MANY WITH HIS HANDS
ON HIS STOMACH LIKE A WOMAN IN LABOR, EVERY FACE
TURNED DEATHLY PALE?"

*JER. 30:6*

What crushes a person? What are those things that come upon us and cause us to double over, making us unable to move or breathe? The imagery in the question above is visceral. A man bent over, grasping his guts with a pale face. Heart attack? Panic attack? A sudden announcement of a termination, a death, or a divorce?

Behind this question is the announcement of release from exile and a return from captivity to a homeland. Of course, a person in prison or captivity does not know if the opening doors indicate release or execution. After a period of imprisonment, hope drains, and there is nothing but fear and dread. Where do we react to God's good word with dread? Where is fear the response to good news?

## "WHY DO YOU CRY OUT OVER YOUR WOUND, YOUR PAIN THAT HAS NO CURE?"

### *JER. 30:15*

I remember my first visit as a fresh young pastor to a young woman, the neighbor of a church member, with terminal cancer. I walked into the room and introduced myself as Don. Her name was Donna. I asked her how she was. She said she had terminal cancer. I foolishly responded, "How bad is it?" With that, she asked me if I had ever done this before. I said, "No." Neither had she, it turned out, and she invited me into a conversation about a condition that had no cure.

How do you converse about something that has no cure? What do you talk about where all advice has failed and all treatments don't work?

"I WILL BRING HIM NEAR AND HE WILL COME CLOSE TO ME—FOR

WHO IS HE WHO WILL DEVOTE HIMSELF TO BE CLOSE TO ME?"

*JER. 30:21*

What is God looking for in a leader? What skill set is required to be used by God? I'm a seminary-trained pastor. I spent years learning Greek and Hebrew, New and Old Testament theology, ethics, church history, pastoral care, and homiletics (how to preach). The church today has academized spiritual leadership into a degreed process, in which students acquire skills and receive grades and diplomas to certify their suitability to lead. But is that all? I don't undermine solid academic achievement. But there is more.

Who will devote themselves just to be close to God? What does that look like practically? How does that work out in daily life? How would your life be different if you lived close to God?

**"I AM THE LORD, THE GOD OF THE WHOLE HUMAN RACE. IS THERE ANYTHING TOO HARD FOR ME?"**

*JER. 32:27*

There are some plans that just seem too big, unreasonably large. When the economy in the USA was going strong, the church I served had a plan for a large capital campaign to reduce the debt and landscape a prayer garden. The overall scope was in the multiple hundreds of thousands of dollars. Then, the real estate market and economy collapsed. People lost their jobs and homes. Money in accounts vanished, and it seemed wise to abandon the plan and focus on survival.

There are some things that just seem too hard to do. Some dreams seem unrealistic, so we pare them back to a more reasonable size and scale and expectations. Is God limited by our limits? Where could God be at work on something much grander than you can imagine?

## "WILL YOU NOT LEARN A LESSON AND OBEY MY WORDS?"

### JER. 35:12

I have had the privilege of serving churches in which there were retired pastors, who were still a part of the congregation. Retired pastors can be such a gift to a new and young (even old) pastor. They can bring wisdom and maturity, insight and humor when things get tough. But one former pastor I knew behaved badly. He had a hard time not being a pastor anymore and would quietly undercut and sabotage my pastoral authority and initiatives. I tried talking with him and telling him what troubled me and what I hoped could heal our relationship. My words tolled off him like Teflon. I was frustrated until another wise (and retired) pastor said, "He's *unteachable*." That word liberated me from the relationship. This pastor was past learning and lived in reacting. He could not be taught.

Are we still *teachable*? Am I able to learn new lessons from God? Is there a growing learning curve in my life as a pastor and believer, or have I too become *unteachable*?

> "WHY BRING SUCH A GREAT DISASTER ON YOURSELF BY CUTTING OFF
> FROM JUDAH THE MEN AND WOMEN, THE CHILDREN AND THE INFANTS,
> AND SO LEAVE YOURSELF WITHOUT A REMNANT? WHY AROUSE MY
> ANGER WITH WHAT YOUR HANDS HAVE MADE, BURNING INCENSE TO
> OTHER GODS IN EGYPT WHERE YOU HAVE COME TO LIVE?"
>
> *JER. 44:7, 8*

The Amish practice a powerful and cruel form of punishment called the ban. When a person violates community rules, the community cuts that person off and ignores them completely. Wow! That's harsh.

But I have seen "cutting off" go on in churches and families in all the places I have served. One family was particularly angry with a staff person and with me for a legitimate reason. But all attempts at confession and reconciliation were rebuffed. Their solution was not just to leave the church I served, but also to stay away from all churches. They would never subject themselves to the possibility of getting hurt by a church again. On one level I understand that, but they also have very young children who are now growing up with no church home, no regular worship, and no community of faith.

What's the positive fruit of cutting others off? What are the costs following generations will pay? Is it worth it?

**"HAVE YOU FORGOTTEN THE WICKEDNESS**

**COMMITTED BY YOUR ANCESTORS?"**

*JER. 44:9*

I visited the Japanese American museum in Los Angeles some years ago with students from the church and their counselors. One of the counselors was Japanese-American. As we toured the exhibit, I was horrified by the displays of the ten internment camps the U.S. had set up to jail Americans of Japanese ancestry during WWII. I did not realize we constructed these ten camps in locations that can only be described as extreme: high elevation, brutally hot summers, and bitterly cold winters. As we silently walked through the exhibit I whispered to him "I'm sorry."

Where do we need to remember the wickedness our ancestors inflicted on others: slavery, racism, xenophobia, anti-Catholicism, sexism…where? No community is pure and innocent. Where have we forgotten?

## "SHOULD YOU THEN SEEK GREAT THINGS FOR YOURSELF?"

### *JER. 45:5*

I confess it. It's deeply embedded in me. I seek great things for myself. For instance, when we had the chance to upgrade our seats on an international flight, I jumped at the opportunity. I loved hearing our particular class singled out for boarding on a special carpet. I loved the attention we received from courteous flight attendants. I relished the food and service they provided during the flight. And I never thought once about those in the other part of the plane, who were crunched together eating out of boxes.

We see it all the time in buffet lines, entering theaters, shopping at store sales, or finding parking spots. When will we stop seeking great things for ourselves and look out for others? What will it take? "You remnant on the plain, how long will you cut yourself?" Jer. 47:5

Did they seriously cut themselves? Why? Why would Israelites resort to cutting themselves? Who cuts themselves? The priest and prophets of Baal cut themselves in front of Elijah on Mt Carmel (1 Kings 18:28). What did that do? It drew attention to their seriousness, their devotion, their pain, and their desire to impress their god, Baal. It didn't work then, and it doesn't work now.

God is neither moved nor impressed by our self-suffering, our self-abuse, our self-torture. In what ways could you be *cutting yourself* to appeal to God?

## "How can you say, 'We are warriors, men valiant in battle?'"

### *Jer. 48:14*

This is a question from God to the warrior-like nation of Moab, whose people were deeply invested in their identity as a tough and warrior people. They were going to lose and be defeated, God said. What will it take for them to let go of that old warrior mythology and let God alone be king?

What mythology do you still carry about in your head about yourself? I still think of myself as a young pastor (and I turned 60 as I wrote this!). Which of your images need to be released: best athlete, beauty queen, top of the class, most talented musician?

**"Was not Israel the object of your ridicule?
Was she caught among thieves that your shake
your head in scorn whenever you speak of her?"**

*Jer. 48:27*

St. Augustine is reported to have said about the church, "I know she is a whore, but she is my mother!" There are those people and institutions we love to ridicule, scorn, and despise. There are political parties for which some people have nothing but harsh words to say. There are people who have done bad things, and are possibly even in jail, who we continue to sharply criticize.

Did Jesus die for them too? Does God not love them because we disagree with them or dislike them? Moab was a nation used by God to punish Israel, but she went too far and hated Israel. Wait a second, God says, Israel is still my child. Who comes to mind that needs to be removed from its place as an object of ridicule?

"HAS ISRAEL NO CHILDREN? HAS SHE NO HEIRS?
WHY THEN HAS MOLEK TAKEN POSSESSION OF
GAD? WHY DO HIS PEOPLE LIVE IN ITS TOWNS?"

*JER. 49:1*

Molek was a particularly cruel religious god. Molek demanded the burning sacrifice of children to appease his wrath. The cost of having Molek as your god meant killing your children. This passage asks a painful question: what price do our children pay for our decisions? What price will our children pay for the way we have mistreated the environment or expanded the debt? What price will our children pay for our marital infidelity or our selfish consumerism?

**"WHY DO YOU BOAST OF YOUR VALLEYS, BOAST OF YOUR VALLEYS SO FRUITFUL? UNFAITHFUL DAUGHTER AMMON, YOU TRUST IN YOUR RICHES AND SAY, 'WHO WILL ATTACK ME?'"**

*JER. 49:4*

The people in the nation of the Ammonites were great growers and traders. Their net worth was enormous, and their valleys were abundant with rich and exportable fruit. They were pretty contented and pretty cocky about their success.

Success can do that. It can make us think we are safe and immune from problems. Who worries about tomorrow with a full refrigerator tonight? Why worry about the future when your investment account continues to grow? Where are the places in which you can be tempted to trust in your riches?

**"IS THERE NO LONGER WISDOM IN TEMAN? HAS COUNSEL PERISHED FROM THE PRUDENT? HAS THEIR WISDOM DECAYED?"**

*JER. 49:7*

The nation of Edom (south of the Dead Sea) was slated for judgment by God, but they would not receive it. Why? Because no one could speak truth to power. There was no wise counsel to critique mislaid plans. Wisdom decayed into patriotic rhetoric. How can wisdom decay today? Where do you need wise counsel to guide your life?

"IF GRAPE PICKERS CAME TO YOU, WOULD THEY NOT LEAVE
A FEW GRAPES? IF THIEVES CAME DURING THE NIGHT,
WOULD THEY NOT STEAL ONLY AS MUCH AS THEY WANTED?"

*JER. 49:9*

There was a common rule in the Middle East called the rule of gleaning. It meant that fields were not harvested down to the bone. Some extras were left in the fields for the poor. There was a margin of safety for the hungry to find food. But the nation of Edom neglected justice and righteousness and had little compassion on the poor. For their greediness, God declared judgment.

Where do you leave margins for others? What do you leave unconsumed so others can live? Who gleans from your fields?

**"IF THOSE WHO DO NOT DESERVE TO DRINK THE CUP MUST DRINK IT, WHY SHOULD YOU GO UNPUNISHED?"**

*JER. 49:12*

There is unrelenting suffering in the world in full color on every news channel. There is suffering from natural disasters, from wars, and from basic human violence. I have become calloused and immune to dead bodies draped with cloth after the latest suicide bombing or mob outrage. Why do I think I must remain immune? If the innocent suffer, why wouldn't I?

**"WHO IS THE CHOSEN ONE I WILL APPOINT FOR THIS? WHO IS LIKE ME AND WHO CAN CHALLENGE ME? AND WHAT SHEPHERD CAN STAND AGAINST ME?"**

*JER. 49:19, 50:44*

As God finished listing the nations upon which he was planning to execute judgment (a long list!), he followed up with a challenging question about who can stand up to him. What shepherd (or spiritual or political leader) can thwart or stop God when he is at work?

We see larger-than-life leaders strutting their power the world over. They seem immense and impervious. Are they? Can they stand up to God? Can we?

"SON OF MAN, DO YOU SEE WHAT THEY ARE
DOING—THE UTTERLY DETESTABLE THINGS THE
HOUSE OF ISRAEL IS DOING HERE, THINGS THAT
WILL DRIVE ME FAR FROM MY SANCTUARY?"
*EZEK. 8:6*

Ezekiel is an incredibly visual book of prophecy. It is the basis for much of the imagery that is used in the book of Revelation. Before this question was asked of Ezekiel, God had shown him a picture of the Jerusalem Temple with an idol in it, an *idol of jealousy*. That idol infuriated God. Why? Why was jealousy so detestable to God? What is it about jealousy that bothers God and gets in the way of our relationship with him?

Isn't jealousy a consuming passion for some thing? Doesn't jealousy blind us to all other realities, because it's all we can think about? Doesn't jealousy actually replace God? Where has jealousy done damage in your life?

**"SON OF MAN, HAVE YOU SEEN WHAT THE ELDERS OF**
**THE HOUSE OF ISRAEL ARE DOING IN THE DARKNESS,**
**EACH AT THE SHRINE OF HIS OWN IDOL?"**
*EZEK. 8:12*

*Doing in the darkness* takes me all sorts of places. We do in the darkness what we do not want anyone else to see. What we do in the darkness satisfies our lusts and passions, our obsessions and addictions. The image gets more pronounced when God describes *each at the shrine of his own idol.* I picture a personally constructed and well-protected shrine I have made for my own selfish pleasure. This is some dark imagery here. What are some of the dark shrines we need to destroy and leave for the light of God?

**"DO YOU SEE THIS, SON OF MAN?"**

*EZEK. 8:15*

There are things I really don't want to see. There are things I don't want to put down in print. There are things in the world around me and in my interior that I would rather avoid naming. But God asks: *do you see this*? Can we see, name and, confess the evil around us, and that in which we participate?

"HAVE YOU SEEN THIS, SON OF MAN? IS IT A
TRIVIAL MATTER FOR THE HOUSE OF JUDAH TO DO
THE DETESTABLE THINGS THEY ARE DOING HERE?
MUST THEY ALSO FILL THE LAND WITH VIOLENCE
AND CONTINUALLY AROUSE MY ANGER?"
*EZEK. 8:17*

What's the detestable thing that God asks if Ezekiel has seen? Is it the men in the Temple facing east and bowing to the sun—what's so detestable about that? Isn't God seen in the rising and setting of the sun? Did God not make all creation to display his glory? Can people both worship God and give honor to the sun? As I see it, it's just a little cultural accommodation to the conditions at the time. It's getting along with the community so the Temple is not marginalized.

Where might we have accommodated to secular cultural practices and values and added them to our faith life? Is it acceptable or detestable?

**"HAVE YOU NOT SEEN THE FALSE VISIONS AND
UTTERED LYING DIVINATIONS WHEN YOU SAY, 'THE
LORD DECLARES,' THOUGH I HAVE NOT SPOKEN?"**

*EZEK. 13:7*

What makes a vision or divination false? Look back at verses 2 and 3. When religious leaders speak "out of their own imaginations" and "follow their own spirit, seeing nothing," a community is in trouble.

The big question I face whenever I prepare to preach is this: *is this my agenda or God's...and how do I know the difference?* The problem is not reserved for ancient people. How can we discern and evaluate our own vision or the vision of spiritual leaders around us? We have a distinct advantage: Jesus. Do the visions and prophesies act consistently with the life and words of Jesus?

## "WILL YOU ENSNARE THE LIVES OF MY PEOPLE BUT PRESERVE YOU OWN?"

### *EZEK. 13:18*

This is a dicey question. The operative verb is *ensnare*, and the focus of God's anger is *women who sew magic charms for wrists* and *veils for heads*. Is this the fashion industry? While these activities Ezekiel witnessed might have been distinctly cultic and religious, what does it mean to *ensnare* a person? What does *snaring* another person look like? Doesn't it mean to stop them in their tracks, get them totally caught up in something and completely preoccupied with *the snare*?

What particularly *ensnares* women today? What *ensnares* men? Are they different? What are you prone to be *ensnared* by?

## "SHOULD I LET THEM INQUIRE OF ME AT ALL?"

### *EZEK. 14:3*

The issue is: should God speak? Elders of Israel came and sat before Ezekiel, acknowledging him as a prophet of God, because they wanted a word from God to them. God had a problem. Should he speak to them? Should he let them inquire of him when (v. 3) "they had set up idols in their hearts and put stumbling blocks before their faces." Are some people not prepared to hear God? Should God *not speak* to some people until some spiritual demolition and preparation is done? What active *idols* and *stumbling blocks* might prevent you from hearing God's voice?

**"SON OF MAN, HOW IS THE WOOD OF A VINE**

**DIFFERENT FROM THAT OF A BRANCH FROM ANY OF**

**THE TREES IN THE FOREST?"**

*EZEK. 15:1-5*

My ancestors were lumbermen in Upper Michigan. They cut down huge white pine forests to supply lumber for expanding America in the late 19th and early 20th century. I have a deep appreciation for forests, wood, and the lumber industry. Though not a woodworker myself, I still enjoy the smells of quality wood that has been cut, milled, and stacked.

I also have grown to love wine and the vineyard culture in both France and California. I have a deep appreciation for what fruit can come from gnarled and twisted vines, tethered to each other by wires and stakes. But the wood of a vine is different than the wood of a maple, oak, or white pine tree. It is valuable for two things: fruit or fire. When it is done bearing fruit, it's ready for the fire. If you were to describe yourself as a type of wood today, what would it be?

## "WAS YOUR PROSTITUTION NOT ENOUGH?"

### *EZEK. 16:20*

Ouch! This is a harsh and damning question. I'd like to avoid it altogether. What is the damage caused by prostitution? Damage is done first to the esteem and health of the woman. Prostitutes are terribly vulnerable to violence, exploitation, abuse, and disease. I would imagine that few prostitutes have healthy relationships with their spouses (if they have them).

What is the further charge God makes to Israel after calling her a prostitute after other gods? He says that she slaughtered her children; she jeopardized the next generation's faithfulness by her own rebellion. She doomed them to a faithlessness spurred by her own faithlessness. But even deeper than what she did to her children was her complete forgetfulness of God. God aches at being forgotten. How is our faith life hurting or helping our "children"?

**"DID YOU NOT ADD LEWDNESS TO ALL YOUR OTHER**

**DETESTABLE PRACTICES?"**

*EZEK. 16:43*

I don't relate to *lewd* and neither, I believe, do you. You would not be reading a daily devotional book of questions from God if you were actively engaged in *lewd* behavior. There would be a cognitive and spiritual dissonance that would be too hard to keep together. So what is *lewd* if we go beyond sexual and moral behavior and see it spiritually? Isn't the essence of *lewdness* total inappropriateness? It's behaving in a way that does not belong; it does not fit or sit well in the environment where it is being practiced. *Lewdness* creates a response of, "What? Ick!" What is *lewd* in our community and culture that needs to go?

"WILL IT THRIVE? SAY TO THIS REBELLIOUS HOUSE, 'DO
YOU NOT KNOW WHAT THESE THINGS MEAN?' WILL HE
SUCCEED? WILL HE WHO DOES SUCH THINGS ESCAPE?
WILL HE BREAK THE TREATY AND YET ESCAPE?"
*EZEK. 17:9, 10, 12, 15*

This series of rhetorical questions all belong to one allegory that begins in Ezek 17:1-8 about eagles and cedar trees, plantings and re-plantings. The center of the question revolves around the word *thrive*. Which plants survive, which plants thrive, and which plants die? What makes faith survive, thrive, or die? What steps have you taken over the years to provide nutrients for your faith, and where have you deprived it? What steps are you sensing that God wants you to take for your faith in him to thrive?

**"WHAT DO YOU PEOPLE MEAN BY QUOTING THIS PROVERB ABOUT THE LAND OF ISRAEL: 'THE PARENTS EAT SOUR GRAPES, AND THE CHILDREN'S TEETH ARE SET ON EDGE?'"**

*EZEK. 18:1*

I grew up in an insensitive culture. It was an all-white, mainly protestant, middle-class community in St. Paul, Minnesota. When Garrison Keillor speaks of the mythical town of Lake Wobegon, I really think he is speaking about my neighborhood. Anybody different was teased: Catholics, Italians, Polish, Irish, African-Americans, Jews, and American Indians. We were the norm, and all others were lesser. We felt bad that they were different than we were, because, somehow, our community was the best, and they could never belong.

That thinking provided a justification for condemnation and approval. Of course they could not succeed. Look what their parents did; they were divorced or some other thing that came with grave social disapproval. That kind of thinking broke for me when we moved to Richmond, Virginia in high school, and I became the minority. It was a painful lesson to learn. Toward which groups of people do you find yourself extra harsh or lenient?

### "Will such a man live?"

*Ezek. 18:13*

One of the dangerous qualities of adolescents (especially boys) is that the part of the brain that understands risks and consequences is not yet fully developed. That's why, according to some psychologists, these boys are the ones who practice extreme sports and are often extremely injured. I saw that when I worked with youth gangs in Chicago. They were genuinely ignorant about the possible consequences of their conduct. They never anticipated that they or their friends would be hurt in any way. A former gang member, who is now a believer, called me some time ago and filled me in on the group: two were in prison, two were dead, two were believers, and he had lost count of a couple more.

There are consequences physically and spiritually—that's reality.

**"'DO I TAKE PLEASURE IN THE DEATH OF THE WICKED?' DECLARES THE SOVEREIGN LORD. 'RATHER, AM I NOT PLEASED WHEN THEY TURN FROM THEIR WAYS AND LIVE?'"**

*EZEK. 18:23*

Chapter 18 of Ezekiel is a tough chapter to read. God sets before Ezekiel conduct and life that yields life and brings death. It seems black and white, cut and dried, and a bit harsh. And one could guess, from the question posed by God to Ezekiel, that God wonders if Ezekiel thinks God likes being cruel. Does God enjoy zapping bad guys and killing the wicked? Does God have a sense of pleasure in removing the evil people from life? No.

God does not put people on a "damnation list" from which they cannot be removed, or remove themselves. The whole point of God's law and warning is for people to turn and live. Whom do you pray for today that needs to turn and live?

**"HEAR, HOUSE OF ISRAEL: IS MY WAY UNJUST? IS IT NOT YOUR WAYS THAT ARE UNJUST?"**

*EZEK. 18:25*

I once received a speeding ticket (in the 1980s in Indiana) and said, "Thank you!" sincerely to the policeman. He looked bewildered because I neither argued nor complained. Why? Because twenty minutes earlier, I was alone on the highway *significantly* exceeding the speed limit in a new car. Had I been stopped at that speed, I probably would have been arrested and the car impounded. So the ticket he gave me was both fortunate and very, very just. I deserved a lot more of a fine than the one I had to pay. (And no, I never drove that fast again.)

Our reflex response to punishment is almost always objection and protest. Who enjoys being caught and punished? Penalties are almost always painful. We often try to get out of "paying" the penalty by objecting that it's just not fair! God's standards and expectations are demanding (what covenant has no demands?), but they are just, aren't they?

## "Have you come to inquire of me?"
### Ezek. 20:3

"What are you doing here?" is a provocative question. It can be, on the one hand, innocent and delightful, said with a smile. It can be businesslike, taking information down about the nature of one's presence (say, in a dentist office). It can be delightful surprise when someone unexpected shows up at church or the front door. Or it can be incredulous and almost indicting, like a casino owner showing up at a Gamblers' Anonymous meeting!

The religious leaders gathered together before Ezekiel. The question was: why were they meeting with Ezekiel? Did they really want a word from God, or did they want to present a word to God? Were they asking or telling, inquiring or opining? Why are you here before God today? Are you here inquiring of him?

## "WHAT IS THIS HIGH PLACE YOU GO TO?"

### EZEK. 20:29

High places don't mean that much in the United States. Height is a numeric designation. High places offer views, and, in urban apartment buildings, cost more than low places. Verticality does not mean that much to the contemporary person.

But, living where we do in southern France and driving through Europe and after spending time in Israel, Greece, and Turkey, I've noticed something about high places: that's where the chateaus and castles are. That's were the fortifications were established, and that's where the powerful and wealthy went—to the high places. The person on the high place controlled (or had access to) power. High places win. High places give people a strategic advantage, insider trading, advanced warning, and set them above the fray.

Where and what are our *high places*, in addition to God, that we go to today to get power and to achieve advantage?

**"WILL YOU DEFILE YOURSELVES THE WAY YOUR**
**ANCESTORS DID AND LUST AFTER THEIR VILE IMAGES?"**
*EZEK. 20:30*

How much of your ancestry do you carry with you? How much of your look, behavior and language reflects your ancestry? I know there are some Michigan/Minnesota-isms in my speech I cannot purge. My wife Martha, when tired, reverts to her softer Virginia accent. There is my Scandinavian love of the woods and the ocean. Some of those ancestral traits are value neutral and just interesting. Other can be spiritually valuable or toxic.

What spiritual traits did your ancestors have that no longer help you spiritually, but in fact hurt you?

## "SHALL WE REJOICE IN THE SCEPTER OF MY ROYAL SON?"
### *EZEK. 21:10*

What does it mean to rejoice in the *scepter*? In this case the *scepter* is neither yours nor mine, but God's royal son (yes, we can think of Jesus). The *scepter* indicates who holds power and authority, and who doesn't (that's you and me). If we get real Christian on this, we say that Jesus reigns right now at the right hand of God (and we don't). What's our job? If we rejoice in the *scepter*, we submit to the one who wields it.

I'm not great at submitting (just ask any church chairperson who told me, "No"). I like consulting and collaborating. I like being asked about things and having my opinions considered. I'm such a democrat (small "d") and believe deeply in democracy. But Jesus' scepter is not democratic. Jesus neither takes votes nor looks at his poll numbers. He reigns. Do we rejoice in his *scepter?*

**"SON OF MAN, WILL YOU JUDGE HER? WILL YOU**

**JUDGE THIS CITY OF BLOODSHED?"**

*EZEK. 22:2*

It's not good to be judgmental, we have all learned. Even though we fight an inner judgmentalism, we try to be fair and impartial. We try to see the other side of things and listen to the other person's point of view. But when God calls out that a city is a city *of bloodshed*, he asks Ezekiel if he would judge that city as God does.

There are those God-judged issues today that God asks us to stand with him in judging: human trafficking of all sorts, abuse of the vulnerable, soul-crushing greed, immorality, and brutal violence. Will we stand with God at those intersections and say, "No"?

**"WILL YOUR COURAGE ENDURE OR YOUR HANDS BE
STRONG IN THE DAY I DEAL WITH YOU?"**
*EZEK. 22:14*

In the community in which I serve in California, I see wealthy people every day. I mean extremely wealthy people. How do I know? I assume it's a wealthy person when the car they drive costs more than a quarter of a million dollars, and the house behind the gates was sold for over ten million dollars. I assume wealth when I see their names listed as benefactors at large gatherings and know they own global corporations. These are genuinely wealthy and powerful people. Some of them behave that way. They give orders and don't take them. They express their views and don't ask others. They are served but do not serve. People attend to them. They are seated right away. These are not bad people, but they are wealthy and powerful. The question that God asks them is *will your courage endure* when it's time to meet with God face-to-face?

That makes me ask myself about all my independence, control, power, and yes, wealth.

**"WILL NOT THE COASTLANDS TREMBLE AT THE**
**SOUND OF YOUR FALL, WHEN THE WOUNDED GROAN**
**AND THE SLAUGHTER TAKES PLACE IN YOU?"**
*EZEK. 26:15*

This is God's question to the nation (city) of Tyre, on the Mediterranean, which was known for its wealth, power, and transportation. They were *the* sailors and sea merchants. Their ships went the farthest and brought back the most goods. I hesitate to mention any city like that today because, in a year or two, it too might fall! Think of the *fallen* cities that were once great—Detroit, Michigan; LA's Inland Empire; Gary, Indiana; Washington, D.C.—and make your own national or global list. We don't look at these former strong cities with admiration, but sadness. They were once great: Beirut, Cairo, Nairobi, and Mexico City. We've seen horrible wars decimate cities like Sarajevo and leave bodies in the streets that once were filled with commerce and families.

What nation, what city, what company, what family, or what person is immune to a great fall?

**"ARE YOU WISER THAN DANIEL?**

**IS NO SECRET HID FROM YOU?"**

*EZEK. 28:3*

This question comes from God to the king of Tyre. In verse 2, God quotes the king as calling himself "a god" sitting on a "throne of god" and thinking of himself as "wiser than god." Success and pride are really dangerous things. There are few times I'm more dangerous than after receiving a compliment that I'm "the best pastor this person has ever sat under!" When I think I'm *that* good, I'm dangerous.

Where is pride also your undoing? Where has pride gotten you in more trouble than you ever imagined? What's God telling you that you are too proud of right now?

### "ARE YOU MORE FAVORED THAN OTHERS?"

*EZEK. 32:19*

I was running through the basement of the church, being chased by another boy. I quickly tossed my Bible onto a shelf and ran into Dorothy, an older woman from the church. "You stop running in the house of God and don't let me *ever* see you throwing a Bible!" Instantly, I went from frightened to angry. "Do you know who I am?" I asked. "I'm Pastor Johnson's son!" She looked right back at me and said, "I don't care whose son you are; I will not tolerate anyone throwing God's word and racing through his church!" I thought I was more favored than that! I wasn't.

Where do you carry a sense of favor or entitlement? What benefits have you earned or have been conferred on you? How has it helped or hindered your spiritual walk with God?

## "How then can we live?"

*Ezek. 33:10*

God asks Ezekiel to ask Israel to ask this question back to God. Circuitous? Yes. Fascinating? Absolutely. Ezekiel (Ezek. 33:1ff) has just been given the job (and curse) of being a watchman for the house of Israel, warning them of coming trouble. And there was going to be downpour of trouble. They seemed doomed to be overwhelmed, judged, and killed. Their list of sins was too great, and they had been rebellious for too long. What's the use, they could easily wonder.

But God was not content; he gave them the question: *How then can we live?* What is our only hope? At the end of the day, what works? The answer is also something God gave: *turn from your evil ways...and live.* Turn from and turn to. Where is any turning going on in your life toward God?

**"WOE TO YOU SHEPHERDS OF ISRAEL WHO**
**ONLY TAKE CARE OF YOURSELVES! SHOULD NOT**
**SHEPHERDS TAKE CARE OF THE FLOCK?"**
*EZEK. 34:2*

I saw a shepherd in the backcountry of France one afternoon. Surrounded by a flock of sheep, carrying a staff, and accompanied by four sheep-herding dogs, he was slowly traipsing through a field. He was there alone, paying attention to the sheep.

I also saw, that same day, in the late afternoon in a little village, several guys huddled around a table, smoking and nursing their beers. They were there together, but for themselves. They were not doing anything particularly wrong, but they were certainly not tending the sheep.

What sheep are you tending? How do you know if you are doing any tending? What does tending look like in your life?

**"Is it not enough for you to feed on the good pasture? Must you also trample the rest of your pasture with your feet?"**

*Ezek. 34:18*

It's called adding insult to injury. It's not only doing something selfish and greedy, but preventing others from enjoying it as well. What comes to my mind is vandalism. There are many abandoned and old buildings and houses in our world. And while it's not legal, it is certainly understandable for a person to find shelter from the weather in these empty places. But why break things? Why punch holes in walls and set fire to pieces of equipment? Why spray paint graffiti and vulgarity on walls?

Where do you see vandalism? Where do you see trampling of the good happening around you? Where might you have done some trampling?

## "SON OF MAN, CAN THESE BONES LIVE?"

*EZEK. 37:3*

There is no clearer image of hopelessness than that of a dry valley filled with scattered bones of men long dead. Bones don't live; people do. Bones depend on so much to be alive. They need to be connected, given tissue and organs, and wrapped in the protective covering of skin. I wouldn't even know where to start.

What are your pictures of hopelessness? How about the one million-person slum of Kibera in Nairobi? How about some of the failed nations in Africa, where marauding soldiers rampantly rape and maim innocent women and children? How about the chronically homeless, mentally ill, and chronically addicted, who litter major urban centers around the world? Where do you see nothing but bones? Where does God direct your gaze?

"IN THAT DAY, WHEN MY PEOPLE ISRAEL ARE LIVING
IN SAFETY, WILL YOU NOT NOTICE OF IT?"
*EZEK. 38:14*

God asks this question through Ezekiel to the larger-than-life enemy nation called Gog. They exist for the destruction of God's people. They are not happy until safe places are trashed and secure places shattered. God seems to ask this question to Gog in an almost taunting fashion. Will you notice when my people live in *safety?* If so, what will you try to do?

Where do you notice the safe places God has created and formed? Where are places of vitality and thriving, where people live in balance and harmony? When we are so surrounded by scandals and bad news, where do we notice the good news?

**"HOW THEN CAN THE LORD PASTURE THEM LIKE**

**LAMBS IN A MEADOW?"**

*HOSEA 4:16*

In verse 15 God called Israel *stubborn, like a stubborn heifer.*
What an image—a rambunctious animal that only wants to run.
Stubborn animals refuse to be led, and they reject care. God
wants to give his people safe pasture, if only they will trust him
and let him lead them.

How do you resist *pasturing* and the care God wants to give
you? Where does your stubbornness get in the way of God's
plans for you?

## "What can I do with you, Ephraim? What can I do with you, Judah?"

### *Hosea 6:4*

He was a friend, classmate, and colleague. But he was a trainwreck. He lived his life so impulsively and out of control, that people refused to work with him if he was on a committee. At the oddest of times he would make outrageous statements and would sabotage the working of almost any group. Deep down he was good guy, but he was fickle and totally unpredictable. You could not count on him to follow through. And sadly, over time, it took its toll on his life.

Ephraim and Judah were fickle and unreliable. They made commitments they did not keep and promises they regularly broke. They were devoted to God one day and off on their own agenda the next. What can God do with fickle people?

## "HOW LONG WILL THEY BE INCAPABLE OF PURITY?"

### HOSEA 8:5

There are a whole bunch of pursuits, hobbies, sports and activities I am *incapable* of doing. I cannot dribble a basketball and walk at the same time (much less have other people intentionally getting into my way). I am incapable of taking apart an engine and ever having it work again. I am incapable of tasks requiring skills in math (decimal points keep shifting places!). These aren't about willingness, rather inability. I can do some things, and I cannot do others even though I have taken lessons (like golf).

But isn't morality and purity built into us? Don't we all have an inner compass that tells us right from wrong and good from evil? Other than the deeply disturbed, don't we know when something is pure or impure? How does a nation become *incapable* of purity? What has to go wrong? Where is it in our day? Where might it be in me?

## "WHAT WILL YOU DO ON THE DAY OF YOUR APPOINTED FESTIVALS, ON THE FESTAL DAYS OF THE LORD?"
### HOSEA 9:5

There are some things I've learned not to mess with. There are some traditions and customs that must go on no matter what. Christmas Eve *needs* "Silent Night" sung, or I will not have a silent night for many nights. On Mothers' Day, a pastor had better acknowledge the loving care mothers have given us, or I'll face some very angry mothers! The Fourth of July (in the USA) needs parades and fireworks, and Thanksgiving needs a big meal, preferably of turkey (again in the USA).

What do we do when these holidays come around, and we are not ready, not prepared, not deserving? How many of us have "faked it" through a holiday just to survive and avoid making waves? Where do we do the same thing with God, dressing up, going to church, and going through the motions, when our hearts are in a foreign place?

## "WILL NOT WAR AGAIN OVERTAKE THE EVILDOERS IN GIBEAH?"

*HOSEA 10:9*

Someone once said that no war ever began with a first shot. By that they meant that no war begins from a ground zero, but it is a justified response to some prior grievance. It is retaliation for a wrong perpetrated shortly or long ago. And few wars are successful, but all create deep seeds of resentment that will emerge years, decades, or even centuries later. Violence begets violence and creates its own punishment.

That's God's question to Israel. While safe at the moment, but spiritually rebellious and unfaithful, will not *war* come back to haunt them again and again? What dictator lasts and dies peacefully? Doesn't God's justice eventually always triumph?

"HOW CAN I GIVE YOU UP, EPHRAIM? HOW CAN I
HAND YOU OVER, ISRAEL? HOW CAN I TREAT YOU
LIKE ADMAH? HOW CAN I MAKE YOU LIKE ZEBOYIM?"
*HOSEA 11:8*

Chapter 11 of Hosea almost makes me weep. It's a father's loving lament over a child whom he loved and who broke his heart. I know too many dads like that, and I know too many children like that, who are estranged and angry with their parent(s) and are sure they are no longer loved—sure that their parents no longer care.

How many people are like that with God? They got angry and were hurt by the church (or by pastors or priests) and they are *never* coming back. They are *never* trusting or believing in God again. What is God's response? See the question above.

**"IS GILEAD WICKED? ITS PEOPLE ARE WORTHLESS!**
**DO THEY SACRIFICE BULLS IN GILGAL?"**

*HOSEA 12:11*

Wicked is as wicked does. Gilead's guilt of being wicked is established by the rhetorical question of what do they do in Gilgal. Sacrificing a bull was something Israel did all the time, not in Gilgal, but in Jerusalem. Alternative places of sacrifice were set up to appease other tribes, other traditions, other gods. Where does God look at our culture and use the word *worthless?* What do we do that really accomplishes nothing?

"WHERE IS YOUR KING? THAT HE MAY SAVE YOU?
WHERE ARE YOUR RULERS IN ALL YOUR TOWNS? OF
WHOM YOU SAID, 'GIVE ME A KING AND PRINCES?'"

*HOSEA 13:10*

When I get _____, then I'll be really happy. When I earn $_____, then I'll be successful and content. When I _____, I'll know I have arrived. Did you ever say or think and of these things? Israel did in I Samuel 8:5, when the people demanded a king like all the other nations. They were sure they were small and insignificant because they were led by a ragged bunch of Judges, who did not garner the respect that a proper king would. And God gave them a king and kings and more kings. But God knew what their demand of a king really meant. It was a rejection of God as King.

Now that you have your king, or _____, or $_____, how's that working out for you? Are you there yet?

**"WHERE, O DEATH, ARE YOUR PLAGUES? WHERE,**

**O GRAVE, IS YOUR DESTRUCTION?"**

*HOSEA 13:14*

The Apostle Paul borrowed this question from Hosea and planted it in I Corinthians 15:55. It's the question asked of death. After you have done your best, O death, what more do you have? God is not timid about naming our deepest fears. Bring on the worst, and put a name to it: Alzheimer's, cancer, failure, poverty, lovelessness, what?

## "EPHRAIM, WHAT MORE HAVE I TO DO WITH IDOLS?"

### HOSEA 14:8

I had a pair of skis I bought in high school with hard-earned money from working at an ice cream store. These were Jean Claude Killy skis made by Head Ski Company in honor of Killy winning three Olympic gold medals in skiing in the 1960s. I kept those skis throughout high school, college, and marriage. Those skis moved with me from Chicago, to Indiana, to Michigan, and finally to Minnesota. They became outdated and non-functioning. I still skied, but I rented new skis the few times I went. Before moving to California, I gave them away to Goodwill Industries, after hauling them around for over thirty years!

What outdated items do you keep carrying around that do you no good at all any more? What do you keep carrying around from long ago that might even look like an idol? Time to let it go?

**"WHO IS WISE? LET THEM REALIZE THESE THINGS.**
**WHO IS DISCERNING? LET THEM UNDERSTAND."**

*HOSEA 14:9*

I am neither a scientist nor an engineer, but I have many friends who are. One friend I knew and greatly respected worked as an engineer on the NASA lunar landing. One day on a long car ride together, he told me step by step what an adventure (and risk) it was to land on the moon and leave again. I listened in rapt silence (and respect) for the engineering and scientific greatness that accomplished that magnificent feat. Part of the source of my respect was that it worked. It was not just a half-cocked theory, but they actually did land men on the moon!

At the end of the book of Hosea, God asked this question about who is really wise. And the deepest proof of wisdom is the same—it works, it really works. "The ways of the Lord are right; and the righteous walk in them." (Hos 14:9b). God's ways are right, and they are wise, because they enable us to really walk. Where does God's way work most in your life?

**"HAS ANYTHING LIKE THIS EVER HAPPENED IN**

**YOUR DAYS OR IN THE DAYS OF YOUR ANCESTORS?"**

*JOEL 1:2*

We look for trends and patterns in the weather, the stock market, fashion, and politics. It seems that if we can find a pattern, we can determine where we are and where we are going. That can be reassuring. If a doctor tells us how both a disease and a treatment will progress, we don't worry when we experience new and uncomfortable sensations. It all fits a pattern.

The book of Joel has a pattern to it, but it's a threatening pattern called *The Day of the Lord*. Joel's task is to announce that things in Israel are fundamentally and uniquely changing, and not all will be good. What's going to happen will be painfully new and disjunctive from anything Israel ever experienced: it's invasion, defeat, destruction, and exile. There was no pattern for this.

Where do you sense God is moving in new and big ways in your life? Where is that exciting, and where is it frightening?

**"HAS NOT THE FOOD BEEN CUT OFF BEFORE OUR VERY EYES—JOY AND GLADNESS FROM THE HOUSE OF GOD?"**
*JOEL 1:16*

My dad loved to eat! While not a gourmand, he loved chocolate, good coffee, ice cream, Pepsi, pasties (a specialty dish of Northern Michigan), and more chocolate. When a feeding tube was put into him at the end of his battle with Parkinson's disease, he lost the taste, smell, and desire for food. He was miserable, and now, with years of hindsight, I wonder if it was worth it? His food was cut off and delivered in a tasteless liquid of nutrition. And when his food was cut off, so was a lot of joy.

Where's your food and where's your joy? How does the house of God bring you deep joy like a great meal does? How does the house of God sustain you like food?

## "THE DAY OF THE LORD IS GREAT; IT IS DREADFUL. WHO CAN ENDURE IT?"

*JOEL 2:11*

We conducted an ocean baptism in February in Santa Barbara. The water was a bit chillier than normal, but the young man wanted an ocean baptism. So his father and brothers, an associate pastor, the young man and I waded out into the water. There were some waves, but not anything to worry about. Then a rogue wave (a wave that was out of the pattern) crested just beyond where we were standing in waist-deep water and tumbled and tossed us head over heels. I grabbed the young man and we did cartwheels together in the surf. You don't endure waves; you either ride them or get tossed.

*The day of the Lord* is more than a wave; it's a tsunami. When it comes, everything in its path succumbs. You don't endure or even ride *the day of the Lord*; you submit to it. Where and how is God calling you to stop resisting him and to submit?

**"Now what have you against me, Tyre and Sidon and all you regions of Philistia? Are you repaying me for something I have done?"**

*Joel 3:4*

Bullies do not like to be bullied. People in power do not like relinquishing power. Those in charge do not like having roles changed. God promised to restore the fortunes of Israel after punishment, but God knew the very instruments, which he used to punish Israel, would resent the restoration of his people and consider Israel's return an affront.

Why is it that some parents resent it when other people's children do well and earn awards? Why do some parents grit their teeth at the achievement of other children? Why is there such competition? Where is God blessing someone you think is unlikely to be a target for his blessing? Why can we be so resentful of God's generosity to others?

**"SHALL I LEAVE THEIR INNOCENT BLOOD UNPUNISHED?"**

*JOEL 3:21*

All bills come due. We live in a world that is paying the price for overspending, under-producing, and borrowing from the future. We have seen nations teeter on the edge of default. We have seen greed and foolishness neglect needs and cater to power and think that they can defer payment off into the future. For how long?

God also has bills he demands payment on. But God is less concerned with national economics than with global justice and righteousness. Where are you aware of innocent blood that God will collect upon?

"DO TWO WALK TOGETHER UNLESS THEY HAVE AGREED TO? DOES A LION ROAR IN THE THICKET WHEN IT HAS NO PREY? DOES IT GROWL IN ITS DEN WHEN IT HAS CAUGHT NOTHING? DOES A BIRD SWOOP DOWN TO A TRAP ON THE GROUND WHEN NO BAIT IS THERE? DOES A TRAP SPRING UP FROM THE GROUND IF IT HAS NOT CAUGHT ANYTHING? WHEN A TRUMPET SOUNDS IN A CITY, DO NOT THE PEOPLE TREMBLE? WHEN DISASTER COMES TO A CITY, HAS NOT THE LORD CAUSED IT?"

*AMOS 3:3-6*

We live in a parsonage adjacent to the church I serve, on the property. For a stressful period of three weeks, the fire alarm went off randomly (at two or three in the morning). Each time I heard the noise from my bed, answered the phone call from the alarm company, and went out to meet the fire department. We had to enter the building with the screaming Klaxon alarm and reset it to silence. The fire department did not immediately leave, but they did a careful sweep of the building for any possible signs of fire, because, maybe, this was not a false alarm. It was finally fixed, and I could sleep again.

When alarms go off and police sirens scream and guard dogs bark...pay attention. Alarms and warning do not (usually) go off without reason. When God warns, we too should pay attention. How do you perceive God's warnings?

**"THE LION HAS ROARED—WHO WILL NOT FEAR? THE SOVEREIGN LORD HAS SPOKEN- WHO CAN BUT PROPHESY?"**

*JOEL 3:8*

When we lived in Chicago, I worked as a youth pastor in a suburb outside the city. That meant I often came home late at night after youth events. One night, while opening the door to the garage, a pack of growling dogs approached me in the alley. I was never more frightened than by their feral and primal growl. They were going to attack me, and I had no weapon. I made it back into my car and drove around the block several times until I was sure they were gone. I took those growls seriously!

Joel calls the Lord's voice like that of a lion's growl. That's a lot more ferocious than dogs! And again, the only appropriate reaction to that sound is self-protective fear.

Where does God's voice growl to you? Where do his words make you shudder? Have we so domesticated God that this very notion sounds weird?

**"WHY DO YOU LONG FOR THE DAY OF THE LORD? THAT DAY WILL BE DARKNESS AND NOT LIGHT. WILL NOT THE DAY OF THE LORD BE DARKNESS AND NOT LIGHT— PITCH-DARK, WITHOUT A RAY OF BRIGHTNESS?"**

*AMOS 5:18, 20*

A danger of being a pastor is overusing vocabulary like "God bless you" and "well, it's in God's hands" or "I'll be sure to pray for you." Often times I am tempted to use well-worn phrases to quickly move away from a person and on to the next thing. Israel bandied about the phrase "day of the Lord" like a trip to Disney Land. When the "day of the Lord" comes, everything will be right, nice, and shiny. What they also thought was that things would eventually turn out their way and for their sole advantage. Really?

How often do we not understand the language of faith and domesticate it to mean something safe? We can sentimentalize Christmas and Holy Week to make it more about kids and food, rather than the trauma of birth and the gore of death. We offer the forgiveness of sins like a sweet and painless bandage, rather than chemotherapy for the soul, almost killing it with the healing medicine. What phrases does God want you to carefully reconsider and use with deeper reverence?

## "DID YOU BRING ME SACRIFICES AND OFFERINGS FORTY YEARS IN THE WILDERNESS, HOUSE OF ISRAEL?"

*Amos 5:24*

I have a friend with an entitled young adult son. This young man regularly berates her for all that she has not done for him and all the things she should be grateful to him for. The problem is that he has neither a degree nor a job and lives on an allowance from home, which he complains is not enough. This scenario is replayed too many times in too many lives. There are too many ungrateful and whiny people, who have yet to grow up and be responsible.

Oh, that sounds like Israel! Amos was sent as a prophet to a proud and cocky people, who thought they ran the show. They were really impressed by the religious spectacle they created in the Temple in Jerusalem. It was the finest production anywhere. It's so good even God weeps! Really now?

The question above looks at the long-repeated story of who carries whom. How quickly we forget the years and the miles God completely carried us.

**"Do horses run on the rocky crags? Does one plow the sea with oxen?"**

*Amos 6:12*

I cringe at the way our culture has euphemized language: pornography is called adult literature, prostitution is called escort service, displacing the poor is called gentrification, greed is called ambition, and firing people is called a market adjustment. We are regularly sold bills of good by marketing campaigns that make wrong look positively attractive. But, in the end, it is as nonsensical as horses running through rocky crags in the mountains or oxen plowing the waves. God is not fooled by the careful packaging of our language.

Where do you sense God's clear call to justice and righteousness in your community?

## "WHAT DO YOU SEE, AMOS?"

### *AMOS 7:8, 8:2*

God gave Amos visions of a plumb line and a basket of fruit. These two powerful images spoke of God's standards for both justice and worship. The problem for Israel was that, over time, their walls leaned in, and their standard changed and adapted for their comfort and profit. They were a market-driven society. Bottom line ruled. And that meant standards of commerce flexed, and Sabbath holiness caved in. What would the plumb line look like across your community? How's our Sabbath in God's eyes?

"WILL NOT THE LAND TREMBLE FOR THIS AND ALL
WHO LIVE IN IT MOURN?"
*AMOS 8:8*

I've been in two earthquakes. As a young man living in Japan, I stood in a doorway for several nauseous seconds as everything moved, shook, and swayed. And in California I was in another church when I thought an especially boisterous bunch of young people were stampeding down the stairs (turns out there were neither young people nor stairs!). When the earth quakes and moves, one's whole frame of reference is disrupted. The stable thing is not stable, and the still thing moves.

When God rights all the wrongs and establishes his justice and righteousness, mercy and truth, what will not shake? What institutions and customs will not have to change?

> "'ARE NOT YOU ISRAELITES THE SAME TO ME AS
> THE CUSHITES?' DECLARES THE LORD. 'DID I NOT
> BRING UP ISRAEL FROM EGYPT, THE PHILISTINES
> OF CAPHTOR AND THE ARAMEANS FROM KIR?'"
> *AMOS 9:7*

Israel knew she was special in God's eyes. God covenanted with Israel long ago through Abraham and many others. He would bless Israel, and through Israel all the nations of the earth would be blessed. Israel had a special relationship with God, and she knew it. But the problem was that Israel extended that special relationship into other areas of life that God did not promise, like exemption from accountability for sin. If I am so special, she thought, God will give me a pass on these sins, these compromises.

While a physician loves her children more than any other children, a broken arm of a daughter is just as serious as a broken arm of a stranger. Being related to the physician does not exempt one from surgery. Where does your relationship with God sometime give you a sense of exemption?

"IF THIEVES CAME TO YOU, IF ROBBERS IN THE NIGHT, OH
WHAT A DISASTER AWAITS YOU- WOULD THEY NOT STEAL
ONLY AS MUCH AS THEY WANTED? IF GRAPE PICKERS CAM TO
YOU WOULD THEY NOT LEAVE A FEW GRAPES?"

*OBAD. 1:5*

The message from the little book of Obadiah is about judgment on Israel for spiritual pride. Pride is our undoing too many times. Pride gets in the way of seeing others in need or seeing our own need for God's grace. Pride insulates us with a scab of mythology that says we really are better than the rest.

The question God asks Israel is about their track record of surviving bad things like robbers who steal, but who still leave some behind, or grape thieves who steal some grapes but not all. Have not most bad things that happened to you, still left some parts of life intact and even stronger than before?

**"'IN THAT DAY,' DECLARES THE LORD, 'WILL I
NOT DESTROY THE WISE IN EDOM, PEOPLE OF
UNDERSTANDING IN THE MOUNTAINS OF ESAU?'"**

*OBAD. 1:8*

God's wisdom is total and his power is unrivaled. God has no consultants or advisors. God does not require a second opinion or further study. With God's wisdom there is no need to say, "Yes, but…" God has the last and final word. There is no appeal beyond God's judgment. How does the finality of God's wisdom give you deep hope?

**"Is it right for you to be angry?"**

*Jonah 4:4*

I love Jonah because he so reminds me of me. He is stubborn and petulant, a reluctant prophet, but, in the end, obedient. He preached the shortest sermon in the Bible: "Forty more days and you will be destroyed!" (Jonah 3:4) Everyone repented and God changed his mind and offered them grace. Oh, that made Jonah mad! Nineveh did not deserve grace but punishment. Jonah thought God was making a big mistake, and he was angry with God.

Anger is a close and unruly relative of mine. Anger is just beneath the surface in my life, and it can erupt at a moment's notice. When anger begins to boil, my calmer sense goes into hiding. God faced Jonah's anger (and ours) with this one question: *is it right?*

## "Is it right for you to be angry about the gourd?"

### Jonah 4:9

As you know in the story of Jonah, God provided Jonah with shade from a gourd plant while he waited for the prophesied destruction of Nineveh. Then God *appointed* a worm to eat the root of the gourd plant, and Jonah was angry again about the loss of his shade and his impending physical discomfort while he waited for destruction to come upon others.

It's as if God asked me if it was right for me to be angry about my Wi-Fi not working or the air conditioning breaking in the car. Anger is dangerous enough when it begins to boil, but the causes of anger are sometimes so trivial that it's embarrassing. Where is God asking you to re-examine the cause of your anger?

"AND SHOULD I NOT HAVE MORE CONCERN FOR THE GREAT CITY
OF NINEVEH, IN WHICH THERE ARE MORE THAN A HUNDRED AND
TWENTY THOUSAND PEOPLE WHO CANNOT TELL THEIR RIGHT
HAND FROM THEIR LEFT—AND ALSO MANY ANIMALS?"

*JONAH 4:11*

The operative words in this question are the two words *more concern*. *More concern* reveals a strategic priority of value, of discerning what is more valuable from what is less valuable, more critical from less critical. My problem is that I can live in a world where every perceived crisis is equally critical, and they are not. A business guide said, "A lack of planning on your part does not make an emergency on my part." Our world screams to us in high volume about too many "emergencies" that are not emergencies at all. In what way does what God have *more concern* about affect what you have more concern about?

**"WHAT IS JACOB'S TRANSGRESSION? IS IT NOT
SAMARIA? WHAT IS JUDAH'S HIGH PLACE? IS IT
NOT JERUSALEM?"**
*MIC. 1:5*

*Dueling Banjos* was a delightful piece of music back in
the 1970s. It consisted of two banjos playing back and forth
together—from simple chords that were echoed back to more
and more complex sounds, rhythms, and speeds.

In Micah's day Israel had dueling Temples: Samaria and
Jerusalem. For long and complicated reasons, Israel (North and
South) had two worshiping centers for two people groups: "pure"
Jews and "mixed race" Samarians. This was not a friendly duel.
They often defined themselves by what they were not and by how
bad the other group was in comparison. Worship was battle and
competition. It's like the sad battles that go on in some churches
between "contemporary" and "traditional" music. There can be
deep rifts, strong feelings, and nasty language. How do those
duels honor God?

"HOUSE OF JACOB, SHOULD IT BE SAID, 'DOES
THE LORD BECOME IMPATIENT? DOES HE DO SUCH
THINGS? DO NOT MY WORDS DO GOOD TO THOSE
WHO ARE UPRIGHT?'"

*MIC. 2:7*

I grew up with a mother who avoided conflict. Conflict made my mother very anxious. So a rule was established at the dinner table of, "No conflict, no disagreement, no touchy topics." When we began to discuss something and the tension began to increase, either my dad or mother would quickly interject, "Let's talk about something else!" The conversation immediately shifted off of the conflict-laden topic to something safer.

God's judgment was a topic of conflict during Micah's day, and the priests around him deemed it too controversial—a topic to be avoided. Stay off of the hot-button topics like sin, repentance, justice, righteousness, and judgment. Are God's words something we can pick and choose from? Do God's words do bad things? Are there areas of the Bible you avoid reading?

"SHOULD YOU NOT KNOW JUSTICE, YOU WHO HATE
GOOD AND LOVE EVIL; WHO TEAR THE SKIN FROM
MY PEOPLE AND THE FLESH FROM THEIR BONES...?"

*MIC. 3:2FF*

This is a deeply troubling question to the leaders of Israel: *should you not know justice?* Isn't an awareness of justice a sine qua non for a national leader, a church leader, or an individual believer? Is justice reduced to a political volleyball that gets batted from left to right, from liberal to conservative, with no objective foundation? Would not a deep awareness of justice make a difference in the way our leaders behave, allocate resources, and enact laws? Pray that God would help you have a deep knowledge of justice in your world.

"WHY DO YOU CRY ALOUD—HAVE YOU NO KING?
HAS YOUR RULER PERISHED, THAT PAIN SEIZES YOU
LIKE THAT OF A WOMAN IN LABOR?"

*MIC. 4:9*

There is the story about the man who fell off a cliff and found a grip on a root. He called out, "God! Help me!" God replied back "I am here son, let go," and the man shouted back, "Anyone else up there?"

When God is in charge, why do we look for a second opinion or someone more familiar (like a king)? Where is God asking you to turn to him as your king and redeemer?

**"MY PEOPLE, WHAT HAVE I DONE TO YOU? HOW**

**HAVE I BURDENED YOU?"**

*MIC. 6:3*

A dark secret among most pastors is that we complain a lot about the congregations we serve and the *burden* it is to be a pastor. We complain about being underpaid and overworked, unappreciated and always the focus of someone's criticisms. There is a lot of whining that goes on when pastors gather. I'd guess the same could probably be said about a lot of believers. If left to ourselves, our conversations devolve into gossip, complaints, and criticisms about our churches, our pastors, and our leaders.

The question God asked Israel is the same one he asks us: how is my gift of salvation a *burden* to you?

**"AM I STILL TO FORGET YOUR ILL-GOTTEN TREASURES, YOU WICKED HOUSE, AND THE SHORT EPHA, WHICH IS ACCURSED? SHALL I ACQUIT A PERSON WITH DISHONEST SCALES, WITH A BAG OF FALSE WEIGHTS?"**

*MIC. 6:10-11*

At a Trustee Board meeting at a church early in my ministry, I naively questioned the ethics of a financial decision the church was contemplating. A very successful businessman put his hand on my shoulder, patting me and saying, "Listen, Pastor, church is church, but business is business." Everyone laughed and went back to the discussion.

Was he right? How has money shaded your sense of right and wrong? Where have you been tempted (or succumbed) to adjusting the weights in your favor? What needs to change?

**"ALL WHO HEAR THE NEWS ABOUT YOU CLAP THEIR HANDS AT YOUR FALL, FOR WHO HAS NOT FELT YOUR ENDLESS CRUELTY?"**

*NAH. 3:19*

Nineveh's repentance after Jonah's preaching did not last. She became a city known for cruelty and misery. Her business practices were harsh, and her power was unkind. Everyone had a "Nineveh story" that they never wanted to experience again. And God announced judgment on Nineveh through the prophet Nahum. I winced at the phrase, *who has not felt your endless cruelty,* and prayed that my face and my name would not be mentioned by anyone before God. What have people *felt* as they encountered me; what have they felt when they encountered you? May they experience God's love and Jesus' kindness through us.

"**WILL NOT YOUR CREDITORS SUDDENLY ARISE?**
**WILL THEY NOT WAKE UP AND MAKE YOU TREMBLE?**"
*HAB. 2:7*

Who can forget the moral train wreck named Bernard Maddoff? He was a high stakes investment trader who made billions of dollars of other people's money in a classic Ponzi scheme. When he went to trial in New York City, his creditors and investors lined the street like angry wolves. He stole their life savings and spent it on high living for decades.

Habakkuk's question from God is to all the rich who made their fortune on the backs of others. If people knew how you got where you are, what would they say and what would they do?

**"HAS NOT THE LORD ALMIGHTY DETERMINED THAT THE PEOPLE'S LABOR IS ONLY FUEL FOR THE FIRE, THAT THE NATIONS EXHAUST THEMSELVES FOR NOTHING?"**

*HAB. 2:13*

What is it for that we labor so hard? What is the reason we get exhausted? In verses 8-12, Habakkuk lists a long litany of projects and schemes in which Israel's rich were engaged. But they always exacted a huge human toll. In the end, was it worth it? Examine the remnants of the latest dictators who have fallen. What did they leave behind? Was it worth it?

**"OF WHAT VALUE IS AN IDOL THAT SOMEONE HAS CARVED? OR AN IMAGE THAT TEACHES LIES?"**

*HAB. 2:18*

My wife is an artist. She knows and evaluates the worth of crafted images (carved, painted, drawn, or printed). Images have value, artistically and creatively. But do they have spiritual worth? The indicting word in the two questions is at the end of the second one: *lies*. What value is a lie? What long-term good does a lie do? How much would you pay for a really good lie to you? Where are we being lied to today? Where are we paying far more than they are worth?

**"IS IT A TIME FOR YOU YOURSELVES TO BE LIVING**

**IN YOUR PANELED HOUSE WHILE THIS HOUSE**

**REMAINS IN RUINS?"**

*HAG. 1:4*

As a long-term pastor, there is a lot about the "emerging" church I find very admirable. It's critique of denominational bureaucracy and power politics is spot-on. Its approach to multi-ethnic worship is admirable. Its embrace of technology is long overdue. But I question the sloppiness of its space. I question the sloppiness of the dress code. When people are content to worship in ugly (not austere, but decidedly unkempt) spaces, what does that tell you about their value of God—especially when they have the finest of new things elsewhere in their lives? Look at your sanctuary and compare it to the best room where you live. What does it tell you about yourself?

"WHO OF YOU IS LEFT WHO SAW THIS HOUSE IN
ITS FORMER GLORY? HOW DOES IT LOOK TO YOU
NOW? DOES IT NOT SEEM TO YOU LIKE NOTHING?"

*HAG. 2:3*

I walked through the streets of Gemena in the Democratic
Republic of Congo in the 1990s, while President Mobutu was still
in power. You could see the outlines of the old colonial splendor:
wide streets and boulevards, big houses with wraparound
porches, and ornate fountains in once beautiful parks. But by
that time it was all in shambles. There was no water, no electricity,
no infrastructure—nothing but a failed state that has, tragically,
remained failed.

How has God lost his glory in our culture, in your community,
amidst your closest friends and family? Where can you see former
glory, and where do you hope to see glory again?

"IF A PERSON CARRIES CONSECRATED MEAT IN THE FOLD OF HIS
GARMENT, AND THAT FOLD TOUCHES SOME BREAD OR STEW, SOME
WINE, OLIVE OIL OR OTHER FOOD, DOES IT BECOME CONSECRATED?...
IF A PERSON DEFILED BY CONTACT WITH A DEAD BODY TOUCHES ONE
OF THESE THINGS, DOES IT BECOME DEFILED?"

*HAG. 2:12, 13*

The question beneath the question is about what spreads
what. Does purity spread purity, or does defilement spread
defilement? Sadly, defilement spreads faster than purity. Bad
news travels faster than good news. Scandals are hotter topics
than faithfulness. It is what it is. What does that mean to us who
*carry consecration* with us? I know there are places I cannot go,
images I cannot see, gatherings I cannot join. What about you?

## "Is there yet any seed left in the barn?"

### Hag. 2:19

Most of us do not have barns. We have garages and sheds maybe, but very few have barns. What does a barn do? A barn stores stuff. A barn is where the equipment is kept out of the weather and where repairs are made. The barn is where the tools are kept. The barn is where hay is kept dry and where animals are sheltered. And the barn is where the seed is kept safe from decay in the weather or consumed by animals. The barn is where the reserves for the future are stored. And seed is all about future—future crops and future harvest.

Is there any seed left in your barn? What does God want you to consider *planting* in this coming season of life?

"**Where are your ancestors now? And the prophets, do they live forever? But did not my words and my decrees, which I commanded my servants the prophets, overtake your ancestors?**"

*Zech. 1:5, 6*

"Where is she/he now?" and, "Whatever happened to _____?" are frequent questions among old friends. Social media has enabled reconnections with friends from childhood. Sometimes it's rewarding, and other times it's shocking. Time takes its toll on our lives, bodies, and faces. As old friends post new pictures on their social media sites, I often think, "Boy! Have they aged!" Of course, I have not aged a bit!

A long look backward can be very revealing and helpful. God is in it for the long haul with us. We can see faithfulness over decades, even centuries. Look back on your ancestors and reflect on God's faithfulness to them and their obedience to God. What worked and what did not?

## "WHAT DO YOU SEE?"

### ZECH. 4:1, 5:2

Seeing does not get old. I see the darkness of the early morning light and a solitary candle as I write. I see the sky go from black to deep blue to bright light as the sun creeps over the eastern horizon. I see branches, once bare, now budding with spring life. I see bursts of yellow and red and green. I see vintners bent over their vines, individually pruning and preparing them to grow. Oh, each new day brings something wonderful to see.

What do I see spiritually? What do I see in the church I serve and the people to whom I am called to serve? What do I see in my own life today? Where am I looking?

## "DO YOU NOT KNOW WHAT THESE ARE?"

### ZECH. 4:5

Zechariah is given a vision, or a dream, by God. It is very visual: a lamp stand, bowls, channels, and trees. To Zechariah, these items are both random and odd. So when God asked him if he *knew* what they were, he said, "No." Zechariah's "no" opened the door for God's explanation of what he saw. What would have happened if Zechariah said, "Oh yeah, I know what those are!"?

How many times do I feign knowledge of something and totally miss the point? How often do I put on the pretense of understanding a conversation and not really get it at all? Not understanding God is the doorway for God to bring wisdom. What do you really not understand today? Where is God waiting for you to say, "No"?

**"WHO DARES DESPISE THE DAY OF SMALL THINGS?"**

*ZECH. 4:10*

This is one of the best questions in the whole Bible. Certainly, the context of Zechariah brings a fuller meaning; but standing alone, the question is eloquent. We are a culture impressed by *big*. Headlines continually trumpet new, big things: purchase prices, salaries, and technologies.

But God works powerfully through the small things: a young virgin, an old priest, the lunch of a child, a staff in the hand, a woman at a well. Ask God to show you and delight you in a small thing today.

"WHEN YOU FASTED AND MOURNED IN THE FIFTH AND SEVENTH MONTHS FOR THE PAST SEVENTY YEARS, WAS IT REALLY FOR ME THAT YOU FASTED? AND WHEN YOU WERE EATING AND DRINKING, WERE YOU NOT JUST FEASTING FOR YOURSELVES? ARE THESE NOT THE WORDS THE LORD PROCLAIMED THROUGH THE EARLIER PROPHETS WHEN JERUSALEM AND ITS SURROUNDING TOWNS WERE AT REST AND PROSPEROUS, AND THE NEGEV AND WESTERN FOOTHILLS WERE SETTLED?"

*ZECH. 7:5-7*

"Enough about you! Let's go back to talking about me!" illustrates our deep selfishness. Left on our own, we really make life all about us: our needs, desires, pleasures, and wants. The selfishness of sin runs amazingly deep. Even our worship can ultimately be all about us. That's what God asked in the question above about Israel's rigorous practice of mourning and fasting, feasting, and sacrificing. Who was it all for, really?

How can we know if our worship is really for God or for us? What is the measuring stick you can use to evaluate the integrity of your worship?

"WHEN YOU OFFER BLIND ANIMALS FOR SACRIFICE, IS THAT NOT WRONG? WHEN YOU SACRIFICE LAME OR DISEASED ANIMALS, IS THAT NOT WRONG? TRY OFFERING THEM TO YOUR GOVERNOR! WOULD HE BE PLEASED WITH YOU?"

*MAL. 1:8*

In the California culture in which I serve, I have noticed an odd thing. Young people show up for church in T-shirts, cargo pants, and flip-flops. But when they go out on a date, they wear nice shirts, dresses, and shoes. What's with that? Why is it okay to be informal (sloppy?) with God but dressed up for a date?

What would what you bring to God say if you brought it to the President or Governor?

"NOW IMPLORE GOD TO BE GRACIOUS TO US.
WITH SUCH OFFERINGS FROM YOUR HANDS, WILL
HE ACCEPT YOU?"
*MAL. 1:9*

Malachi is all about cheapness. It's a book that exposes the stinginess of Israel in the face of the generosity of God. A question that I ask couples as they prepare for marriage is, "Who taught you generosity? Who taught you to give?" It's an incredibly revealing question. Some people immediately come up with a name or names of generous persons in their lives who practiced giving. Others stare at me blankly with no names, no generosity, no giving. They came from selfish families who gave begrudgingly and complainingly. Who taught you generosity?

**"WHEN YOU BRING INJURED, LAME OR DISEASED
ANIMALS AND OFFER THEM AS SACRIFICES, SHOULD I
ACCEPT THEM FROM YOUR HANDS?"**

*MAL. 1:13*

"Regifting" is a neologism for our age. It's the practice of passing on a gift that has been given to you as a gift to someone else. On the one hand, it makes sense if you have two of some item, or if you know that another person would really enjoy that item. But it is also cheap and petty, a way of avoiding spending your own money and getting rid of something you never wanted in the first place. What does God get from you?

**"BUT WHO CAN ENDURE THE DAY OF HIS COMING?**

**WHO CAN STAND WHEN HE APPEARS?"**

*MAL. 3:2*

What have you *endured* in your life so far? What sorts of trials have you successfully made it through? Some have gone through cancer, childbirth, divorce, or joblessness. Others have endured graduate school or long apprenticeships. Still others have endured war or violence. Endurance is a highly valued quality in the human spirit. We admire people who have endured great obstacles or challenges. But do you endure God? Can you endure God? What does our endurance have to do with God? Is it an asset or a deficit?

# 2ND ANGEL QUESTION

**"MEN OF GALILEE, WHY DO YOU STAND HERE
LOOKING INTO THE SKY?"**

*ACTS 1:11*

It's amazing what looking does to me. I look at the clock to
know what time it is and what I need to be doing next. I look
outside at the sky to know how to dress for the day. I look at
my bank balance to know how much I can spend. I look at the
church budget and attendance numbers to know if I am doing
a good job leading the congregation. I look at me medical tests
with my physician to know if I'm going to live a while longer and
if I am in good health. I look at all sorts of things. And what I see
often prompts very distinct behaviors and responses.

Why are you looking where you are looking today? What is it
that you see, and what are you looking for? How is your looking
a reflection of your discipleship and faithfulness?

# PART II:
# QUESTIONS FROM JESUS

**"IF YOU LOVE THOSE WHO LOVE YOU, WHAT REWARD WILL YOU GET? ARE NOT EVEN THE TAX COLLECTORS DOING THAT? AND IF YOU GREET ONLY YOUR OWN PEOPLE, WHAT ARE YOU DOING MORE THAN OTHER? DO NOT EVEN PAGANS DO THAT?"**
*MATT. 4:46, 47 (LUKE 6:32-34)*

The most segregated hour of the week is between eleven o'clock and noon every Sunday morning. Or at least, that is the saying out there. (Whether it is an actual truth is irrelevant.) What is true is that we like to hang together; I like to see those people I already know and already like. I like to hang around those people who like to hang around me. I accept people who have already accepted me. And the older I get, the harder it is to break out of my relationship circles.

What makes the church any different from another club? What makes us different from closed clubs with strict membership standards? It should be that we love those who adamantly refuse to love us back. It should mean that we don't give up on those who have given up on us. It should mean that we reach out in love to people who are nothing like us and will never help us advance our agendas.

Dare to ask God today to show you and lead you to someone completely new.

"IS NOT LIFE MORE IMPORTANT THAN FOOD, AND
THE BODY MORE IMPORTANT THAN CLOTHES?
...ARE YOU NOT MUCH MORE VALUABLE THAN
THEY? CAN ANY ONE OF YOU BY YOUR WORRYING
ADD A SINGLE HOUR TO YOUR LIFE? AND WHY DO
YOU WORRY ABOUT CLOTHES?"
*MATT. 6:26-28 (LUKE 12:25)*

For many of us, worry is both an art form and a sport. We love to worry. We worry about the weather, the economy, politics, health, and travel. We worry about what we can never control. And when we are done with a worry episode, we take a break and soon return to worrying about it again with renewed vigor. Some of the things we worry about are so trivial: clothes, food, cars, and material possessions.

Unfortunately, our culture has made the sources of our worry into industries in and of themselves. They have elevated these things to realms of penultimate importance, when, in fact, they are not vital. Worry is gender neutral. Men can criticize women for worrying about one thing, but men can worry about different things with just as much fervor. And, why? At the end of a worrying session, what is accomplished?

What worry does accomplish is to divert us from important things to trivial things. When that happens, Satan and all his minions delight because my energy is now consumed and won't get in his way. Worry leads us down a road of distraction to the neighborhood called irrelevant. And as long as we hang around that neighborhood, we will not be active in the neighborhood of the kingdom of heaven. Ask God to show you where you are worrying unnecessarily.

"IF THAT IS HOW GOD CLOTHES THE GRASS OF THE
FIELD, WHICH IS HERE TODAY AND TOMORROW IS
THROWN INTO THE FIRE, WILL HE NOT MUCH MORE
CLOTHE YOU- YOU OF LITTLE FAITH?"
*MATT. 6:30*

I accidentally closed my hand around a chestnut seed husk.
Ouch! That barbed little thing left painful needles all over my
palm, and it itched for days. Just a dumb chestnut husk! Yet,
as I reflect on this question from Jesus, I confess that God
magnificently provides for the protection and distribution of
chestnut seeds through that elegantly engineered husk that
"bites" all those who try to pierce it. God provides in so many
ways. All it takes is a long walk in the woods to see the multiple
ways God takes care of the "grass of the field."

When I get all wrapped up in myself, it helps to go outside
and actually look at the grass of the field, the birds in the air, and
the flowers all about. Ours is a world of excessive beauty and
color. If God provides all of that, what am I worrying about?
Wherever you are today, in whatever season it is that you read
this, identify five things of beauty around you in nature upon
which you might contemplate and reflect.

"WHY DO YOU LOOK AT THE SPECK OF SAWDUST IN SOMEONE ELSE'S EYE AND PAY NO ATTENTION TO THE PLANK IN YOUR OWN EYE? HOW CAN YOU SAY, 'LET ME TAKE THE SPECK OUT OF YOUR EYE,' WHEN ALL THE TIME THERE IS A PLANK IN YOUR OWN EYE?"

*MATT. 7:3,4 (LUKE 6:41,42)*

The answer to this question is really easy. I see sawdust in your eye because I don't have any good mirrors around me. Simple. If I'm not looking at myself, I must be looking at you. As long as I stay out of range of mirrors, the only faces and eyes I'll see are yours.

A consultant once told me that if you cannot find four legitimately good qualities in an unsatisfactory employee, you are not paying attention. Everyone has good qualities in addition to areas that need improvement. But we have become a monochromatic culture that defines others as good or bad...for me. You are either my friend and I see no wrong; or you are my enemy and I see no good. And I am always right in my own eyes.

Any spirituality without the capacity to self-critique (or confess) is a shallow and dangerous spirituality. It will allow for the polarization of communities into friends and enemies, with me or against me. The solution to this condition of spiritual blindness is a good mirror called confession. Read Psalm 51, and let God fill in the blanks.

**"Do people pick grapes from thorn bushes, or figs from thistles?"**

*Matt. 7:16*

As I write this, I live in southern California where there are abundant fruit trees. In fact, in our backyard are two trees: one apple and one orange. It is very simple to tell the difference between the trees, especially when they are loaded with fruit.

In warning the people about false prophets (read: abusive and self-serving religious authorities), Jesus invites his listeners to just take a look at the "fruit" of their lives and conduct. Everyone has fruit. Everyone's life yields a consequence of life-long behaviors and lifestyle choices.

As a young seminary student, I once went with a professor to a large book fair. It was a delightful experience until he became frustrated and yelled angrily at a vendor. Something changed as I watched that "fruit" drop. I lost respect for him from that day forward. No matter how eloquently he could lecture on intricate matters of theology, he had an uncontrolled mean streak.

What fruits do they see in our lives and behavior? What are the thorns and thistles we bear? Ask God today to both make you aware of others, and prune from you that which does not bear kingdom fruit.

## "SHALL I COME AND HEAL HIM?"

### MATT. 8:7

Jesus does not act passively. Jesus traffics in the explicit. In the story surrounding this question, a Roman soldier, a centurion, who had a very sick servant, informed Jesus about his problem. That should have been enough for Jesus to volunteer to go heal him, but Jesus did not immediately go. Instead he asked the centurion the question above. Why?

Jesus needs to be invited. Jesus needs to be asked. Jesus does not push his way into our lives but comes when we want him and need him. In fact, the issue is more about the centurion's need for Jesus than the servant's need, though the servant was physically ill. The centurion was used to others following his orders and whims. Jesus was not in his chain of command; he was not accountable to him.

So the centurion made a dramatic confession of faith in Jesus that would not have been made if Jesus immediately went. When we intercede on behalf of others, do we go far enough and ask Jesus what we want him to do? What kind of healing or touch are we asking Jesus to make? Too many of us ask Jesus to "bless" another person, but what does that mean really? Is that our quick way of unloading another person into Jesus' lap without really asking him? What specifically do you want Jesus to do for others around you today?

**"WHY DO YOU ENTERTAIN EVIL THOUGHTS IN YOUR HEARTS? WHICH IS EASIER TO SAY, 'YOUR SINS ARE FORGIVEN,' OR TO SAY, 'GET UP AND WALK?'"**

*MATT. 9:4, 5*

Which is the real question; the one about evil thoughts in hearts or about which is easier to say? Why does Jesus tie these together? I like the word for *entertain* in the Greek, which is *en thumos*, or to hold with passion and feeling. Evil thoughts are not in our hearts by accident or mistake. We hold them there intentionally, entertaining them so they feel comfortable. We go back to them over and over with beverages and appetizers to keep them at home.

We get used to evil thoughts as thought they are frequent and regular houseguests: *Oh, there you are! Welcome back!* Jesus was aware of the teacher of the law's evil thoughts—constant suspicion and cynicism. It's the "Oh, sure!" type of reaction we have when we see anything wonderful or new or too good to be true. We doubt integrity, veracity, or motive. It's a trick, a con, or a set up. Not me! I won't believe that stuff!

Jesus challenges their hearts with proof. Which is easier: inner change (sins are forgiven) or outer change (get up and walk)? Do we actually believe that others can be fully forgiven and changed by Jesus? Look again at the thoughts your heart entertains.

## "HOW CAN THE GUESTS OF THE BRIDEGROOM MOURN WHILE HE IS WITH THEM?"

### MATT. 9:15

Bridegrooms are funny guys. Since I've officiated over 400 weddings, I've had the chance to observe many bridegrooms. In fact, I've watched bridegrooms more closely than brides because the bridegrooms traditionally wait to enter the wedding service with me. And often, while the groomsmen are acting as ushers and running around, the bridegroom is sequestered in my office to wait for the others. And for many of them, that's what they've gotten used to doing during the engagement and wedding planning process: patiently waiting and approving their brides' choices of material, food, design, etc. They get used to standing alone and waiting, until the time comes for me to escort him into the sanctuary. And all eyes are on the bridegroom. From that point on, everyone knows where he and she are. The bridegroom and bride are the center of attention until the last guest leaves. It's a fun transformation to watch.

How could cleanup begin when the bridegroom is still at the party? How could sadness start before the party ends? Wedding parties are hard to end. People enjoy the food and festivity as long at the couple is still in attendance.

But have you noticed that at some parties, there is always someone who is hurrying to clean things up and get done with the party so they can go back to their lives and their homes? These are the ones who take plates away from guest before they are finished eating and start putting away the food before everyone has come back for seconds. These are ones who are extremely practical and utilitarian. Party, laughter, joy, praise, and worship are luxuries in which they do not participate. Which kind of guest are you?

## "Do you believe that I am able to do this?"

### Matt. 9:28

This is a question Jesus asked to the blind men, who called out for mercy. Then Jesus invited them indoors for privacy. These blind men had been asking for "mercy" all their lives. What did "mercy" translate into? Money, alms, food, help. Is this what they were asking for again? What else did they know? Did they really want to see? What would that mean?

Are Jesus' words and actions truly life changing and miraculous, or are they simply good advice and helpful tips for living better. Are his words supplementary to what we already know how do to perfectly well on our own (asking for mercy), or will we believe that they can fundamentally alter our existence? What do you believe Jesus can do for you today?

## "WHAT DID YOU GO OUT INTO THE WILDERNESS TO SEE? A REED SWAYED BY THE WIND?"

### MATT. 11:7 (LUKE 7:24-26)

John the Baptist was a piece of work! You could not miss him wherever he went. His wild (probably dreadlocked) hair and mangy coat stood out like a bright light. His eating habits (locusts & honey) were, to say the least, unique. His ranting and raving about sin and repentance was almost a theatrical spectacle—street theater in the wilderness. He certainly knew the Bible and quoted it freely. If you had nothing else to do on a hot afternoon, this could be entertaining. Or was it more?

Jesus' question was to the crowds who had gone to hear John. Some of them had gone into the Jordan River for baptism. And now they were hearing the teaching of Jesus. Beyond the spectacle and show, Jesus asked, what were you going to see? What drew you to such a weird man? Not the "reed swayed by the wind," but your sense of sinfulness and needing forgiveness, your sense of being lost and wanting to be found.

When you go to church, what are you going to see? Friends? A good speech? Nice music? What's behind or underneath the surface of your motivation?

"HAVEN'T YOU READ WHAT DAVID DID WHEN
HE AND HIS COMPANIONS WERE HUNGRY?...OR
HAVEN'T YOU READ IN THE LAW THAT THE PRIESTS
ON SABBATH DUTY IN THE TEMPLE DESECRATE THE
SABBATH AND YET ARE INNOCENT?"

*MATT. 12:3-5*

One of the things Jesus was in hot water for among the religious leaders of his day was his seemingly flippant treatment of all the rules and regulations about observing and honoring the Sabbath. The problem for Jesus was that their critique was dishonest and a consequence of poor scholarship. For the sake of the current tradition of Sabbath compliance, they lightly disregarded both the conduct of King David and the regular tasks of temple priests.

The question of *haven't you read* is indicting. How much of what we currently believe and practice is genuinely based on what we have read in Scripture? Is your practice and theology based on what you have read, or what you have grown familiar doing? Want a test? When was the last time something you read in Scripture changed the way you believe?

"IF ANY OF YOU HAS A SHEEP AND IT FALLS INTO A
PIT ON THE SABBATH WILL YOU NOT TAKE HOLD OF
IT AND LIFE IT OUT?"
*MATT. 12:11 (LUKE 13:15, 14:5)*

What are the limits of what you do and don't do on the Sabbath? For most of us, there are no limits. Sabbath (or Sunday) is just another weekend day off, with occasional time spent in church. However, we do the same things we do on every other day: shop, pay bills, do laundry, clean, run errands, do yard work, etc.

But in Jesus' day Sabbath regulations were so strict and complex that you spent your time and energy contemplating the negative: what you could *not* do or attend. Jesus was not so bound. He regularly and freely healed people of non-emergency diseases on the Sabbath. Why? To irritate the religious leaders? No. Jesus exercised positive energy and acts on the Sabbath as consistent with God's will. What positive acts have you done and will you do this Sabbath?

> **"IF SATAN DRIVES OUT SATAN, HE IS DIVIDED AGAINST HIMSELF. HOW THEN CAN HIS KINGDOM STAND? AND IF I DRIVE OUR DEMONS BY BEELZEBUL, BY WHOM DO YOUR PEOPLE DRIVE THEM OUT?"**
> MATT. *12:26, 27 (LUKE 11:18, 19)*

It's easy to be a critic. It's easy to point out faults and problems in others. It's especially easy to be critical when something (or someone) is different than you. I wrote many of these comments while on sabbatical leave in France. I found it very easy to have an immediately critical reaction to the way the French do things differently than I do them in the USA. For instance, the French break their bread and leave it on the table (as opposed to on the plate where food is *supposed* to be); they serve their meals one course at a time over hours (as opposed to loading up a plate and eating it all at once in 20 minutes); they close their businesses every day from noon to two o'clock, thus eliminating the ability to run noon errands or do grocery shopping. But guess what? They have been doing this for years and years successfully. People are fed, crumbs are cleaned up, and shopping does get done.

Jesus' critics did not like the way he spontaneously healed people and cast out demons. He did things so differently than they did. They had rules and protocols, a clean process with deliberate steps. He just healed people on the street. That's not the way to do things! It must be evil.

Isn't it interesting how easily we can vilify someone who does things differently than we do? Jesus asked them (and us) to look at the outcome. If people are healed of Satan (Beelzebul) by Satan, he must be schizophrenic! Today who do you need to stop criticizing and start praying for instead?

**"YOU BROOD OF VIPERS, HOW CAN YOU WHO ARE**

**EVIL SAY ANYTHING GOOD?"**

*MATT. 12:34*

What's the difference between the purr of a cat and the hiss of a snake? There is a profound difference. One invites and one warns. One is friendly, and the other is dangerous. We instinctively know that and react accordingly.

Who does the hissing today? Where does that sound of snakes come from in your world? What is the source of constant negativity and toxic words and language? There are people I know who consistently hiss. Over the years I have tried to fool myself into thinking that they were just having a bad day and would purr pretty soon. They never did. They consistently hissed and sometimes bit. While not going so far as calling them evil, I have learned to heed the warning of hissing snakes.

**"WHO IS MY MOTHER, AND WHO ARE MY BROTHERS?"**

*MATT. 12:48 (MARK 3:33)*

The call and demand of family is pretty strong. I know who my family is. When any of my kids or wife calls on my cell phone, it sounds a distinct ring, and everyone I work with knows I will stop what I'm doing to answer the call of family. I used to call my dad every week. Even during his working years, he always took my call and was never too busy to talk.

But is there a higher call than family? What happens when obedience to God and family loyalties clash? What happens when children leave (or ignore) the faith? Jesus demonstrates his higher calling to obey God over blood kin. Who is your faith family today? Sometimes they are one and the same. Sometimes they are different.

### "Have you understood these things?"

*Matt. 13:51*

I was conducting premarital counseling with an eager young couple. They young man was extremely nervous about being with a pastor. He had not been in a church for years and felt the need to prove himself to me. So whenever we covered a point, he shot back at me, "Got it!" as if to say, "Okay, move on." He was so anxious to get out of my office, he pushed his sense of understanding what I was talking about, and he didn't *get it*. And on the wedding day he was such a nervous wreck that I had to practically hold his hand to get him through.

In our question above, Jesus has just finished a series of teaching lessons on what the Kingdom of Heaven is all about through parables. Seeds and weeds sowed, mustard seeds, yeast, treasure hidden in a field, searching for pearls, and fishing—get it? On the one hand they are simple and we are tempted to quickly say, "Got it!" But do we understand these parables together?

**"YOU OF LITTLE FAITH, WHY DID YOU DOUBT?"**

*MATT. 14:31*

Peter has just made a major commitment to Jesus. In a storm, believing Jesus was outside the boat, Peter left the safety of the boat to walk to Jesus. No other disciple dared do this. Peter acted on pure faith as he walked on water toward Jesus. Then, he saw the waves and what he was doing, had a moment of doubt and started to sink. Jesus reached out and grabbed his hand, restoring him to water-walking and asked why he doubted.

I wonder why he believed as he did. Why didn't any other disciples join him? Where was the doubt Jesus was asking him about?

**"AND WHY DO YOU BREAK THE COMMAND OF GOD**
**FOR THE SAKE OF YOUR TRADITIONS?"**

*MATT. 15:3*

What are some of your most long-standing traditions? What traditions are so engrained in you that you do them without thinking? Standing for the National Anthem? Putting your hand over your heart for the pledge of allegiance? Opening Christmas gifts on Christmas Eve or morning? Mother's Day brunch? What? Where does God's Word trump your traditions?

## "ARE YOU STILL SO DULL?"

### *MATT. 15:16*

Jesus has just explained to his disciples that there are no exterior things that can cause spiritual pollution. In the face of all the Jewish dietary and washing laws, Jesus said that uncleanness is a matter of the heart not the body.

Peter wants further explanation. And Jesus asked this question: *are you still so dull?* What's dull about Peter's question for clarification? Why does Jesus call this dull? Is it bad to ask Jesus questions, or is Peter asking a follow-up question to avoid understanding the implications of Jesus' teachings? When have we heard enough, and it's time to act? When are our questions masks for either dullness or fear?

## "HOW MANY LOAVES DO YOU HAVE?"

### MATT 15:34

Who admits to being overpaid? Who believes they have enough saved for retirement? Most of us live in constant uncertainty if we will have enough. Some people I know have a hard time spending money on gifts for others because they are so afraid they will not have enough for themselves. The disciples felt that way as Jesus showed compassion for the crowd after a full day of teaching. You can't be serious, Jesus! That's a huge crowd, and we are just twelve poor men. We can't, we don't, there's not enough, they are too many. The needs around us on any given day are far greater than our resources. The truth is we don't have enough.

But Jesus asked the question: *how many do you have?* He wants a number, a finite and distinct number. Many of us don't want to answer that question: *How much do you earn in a year? How much do you have in your account right now? How much cash do you have on you right now?*

**"YOU OF LITTLE FAITH, WHY ARE YOU TALKING AMONG YOURSELVES ABOUT HAVING NO BREAD? DO YOU SILL NOT UNDERSTAND?"**

*MATT. 16:8, 9*

All it took was one little word for the disciples to go off on a tangent: *yeast.* Jesus warned them of the *yeast* of the Pharisees and Sadducees, and the disciples started thinking about dinner plans.

How many times has your thought life been spun off on a tangent completely unrelated to the present moment: someone's clothing at church, the type of music played in worship, an announcement about an event you did not approve, or whatever? How many times have we missed the heart of a message because we got ourselves spun off on a tangent?

## "WHO DO PEOPLE SAY THE SON OF MAN IS?"

### MATT. 16:13 (MARK 8:27, LUKE 9:18)

What's the word on the street today about Jesus? Who do the people you live with and work with say Jesus is? If I'm honest, I have to admit that I don't know because I have not asked them. I hang around believers so much of the time, I'm not sure what other people are saying about who Jesus is. I'm promoting the programs and managing the affairs of the church so much, I'm not listening much to non-believers.

Think about the five non-believers you have a first-name relationship with. Who do they say Jesus is? If you don't know, is now the time to ask them and just listen?

**"BUT WHAT ABOUT YOU, WHO DO YOU SAY THAT I AM?"**
*MATT. 16:15 (MARK 8:29, LUKE 9:20)*

Talk about a direct question! Yikes, this is an awkward one. I love to talk about people to other people, but find it difficult to talk to people about themselves. It seems too direct and uncomfortable. I like to talk about safe things, events and things. To tell you who you are to me is hard, especially because I'm not even sure at times.

This question from Jesus requires an intimate and direct response of *you are_____ to me.* What's your answer in one sentence?

**"WHAT GOOD WILL IT BE FOR YOU TO GAIN THE WHOLE WORLD, YET FORFEIT YOUR SOUL? OR WHAT CAN YOU GIVE IN EXCHANGE FOR YOUR SOUL?"**
*MATT. 16:26 (MARK 8:36, 37, LUKE 9:25)*

Immediate gratification versus long-term gain—that's a daily negotiation for many of us. We want to win. We want to look good and to gain recognition. We want to make money and to be successful. We want...but at what price? Where has your soul ever been on the chopping block in order to make a deal? Do you ever avoid telling the whole truth? Have you undercut a colleague to get a promotion? Do you look the other way when people around you bend the rules? Do you ignore racisms or sexism? Do you laugh when a bully does his/her thing on someone? Where do you draw the line?

## "How long shall I stay with you? How long shall I put up with you?"

### *Matt. 17:17 (Luke 9:41)*

First of all, whom is Jesus talking to and inquiring about—the gathered crowds or the unsuccessful disciples? To the crowds, Jesus' question could be clearly phrased: *how many more miracles do you require for belief to take hold in your lives?* But to the disciples he could have been asking: *what's it going to take for you to face up to evil with prayer?*

When I look at myself in the mirror, a pastor for over 30 years, I wonder if Jesus is just putting up with me or enjoying me?

**"WHAT DO YOU THINK, SIMON? FROM WHOM DO THE KINGS OF THE EARTH COLLECT DUTY AND TAXES—FROM THEIR OWN CHILDREN OF FROM OTHERS?"**

*MATT. 17:25*

A pastor friend used to tell me, "When people say 'it's not the money, it's the principle'...it's really the money!" Money— getting, holding, spending, and paying it—consumes huge amounts of energy. Jesus was being ambushed by a question about taxes. His ministry operated on a slim margin. If they paid taxes, little would be left for ongoing needs. You can sense the tension in the air. Behind this question is the question: *why do we let money grip us so strongly?*

"WHAT DO YOU THINK? IF A MANS OWNS A
HUNDRED SHEEP, AND ONE OF THEM WANDERS
AWAY, WILL HE NOT LEAVE THE NINETY-NINE ON
THE HILLS AND GO TO LOOK FOR THE ONE THAT
WANDERED OFF?"

*MATT. 18:12*

Who gets your attention on a Sunday at church—old friends, newcomers, or absentees? I love having friends greet me and bless me. I like being known and loved, and I find deep comfort in the familiar. Newcomers are tougher because I don't necessarily know how they will react or respond. They might be critical or ask a tough question. So I have to push myself to the newcomers, the visitors. But absentees…yikes! They get me mad.

Why aren't they here? Don't they know this is their church, and I'm their faithful and hardworking pastor? What's wrong with them? Are they going somewhere else, to a better church with a more inspiring pastor? Oh, you'd be amazed at the web of critical assumptions I can spin about those not here. And when someone tells me that they are hurt, wounded, upset, or angry, then I really don't want to go to them and get bawled out. Yet, they have wandered away. Where are they? Who will go to them? Who will look for them? You?

## "Shouldn't you have mercy on your fellow servant just as I have had on you?"

### Matt. 18:33

This question follows the crazy parable of the man who owed 10,000 talents. One talent was one year's wage. Take whatever number you want for a yearly wage (try your own), and multiply it by 10,000. It is just not repayable…ever! The master forgave that crazy debt, and the guy goes and imprisons a man who owed him 100 day's wages.

Why can't the forgiven man be forgiving? What can't grace extend through the person who received so much grace? Why are we so stingy with the grace words like *I'm sorry, you're forgiven, I love you?* As long as Christians hold grudges against other Christians, why should anyone want our faith?

"HAVEN'T YOU READ THAT AT THE BEGINNING THE CREATOR 'MADE THEM MALE AND FEMALE, AND SAID, 'FOR THIS REASON A MAN WILL LEAVE HIS FATHER AND MOTHER AND BE UNITED TO HIS WIFE, AND THE TWO WILL BECOME ONE FLESH?' SO THEY ARE NO LONGER TWO, BUT ONE. THEREFORE WHAT GOD HAS JOINED TOGETHER, LET NO ONE SEPARATE."

*MATT. 19:4-6*

Divorce is epidemic. Too many couples live together before marriage. First marriages are routinely called trial marriages for a couple years. Partners cheat. Love grows cold. What are we missing? What have we forgotten? Is the oneness of marriage an emotional, sexual attainment, or is it a spiritual reality we grow into more and more over the years? Maybe we need to go back and read Genesis 1 and 2 again.

**"Why do you ask me about what is good?"**

*Matt. 19:17*

The good thing. The magic bullet. The secret formula. The secret handshake. "What's the deal, Jesus?" the man asked. "I've tried all sorts of tactics, but what's the formula for eternal life? What new routine do I need to practice to gain immortality?" Is he shopping or what? This guy is a spiritual pilgrim and wanderer, always looking for more.

Before Jesus gives him the tough word about his possessions, he asks him: *why me?* Why have you come to Jesus? Why do you ask Jesus?

## "WHAT IS IT YOU WANT?"

### MATT. 20:21

"Promise not to tell Dad?" I would plead with my mom. It was usually something I did that I knew warranted punishment: bad grades, a broken item, an action that would be reported back to my dad. My mom never bit. She refused to agree to my request sight unseen. She would not have her honesty with my dad compromised.

Two disciples wanted a favor, but Jesus wanted to know specifically what they wanted. He wanted them to name out loud their request, their desire, their hope, their aspiration. What do you want from Jesus today?

## "Can you drink the cup I am going to drink?"

### *Matt. 20:22*

A friend of mine was an airline pilot, who flew an experimental and aerobatic plane. He took me for the most thrilling ride of my life, looping and spinning and turning the whole world around for me with apparent effortlessness. I loved it. But, I did not want to invest the thousands of hours it would take to be a pilot like him. I was not willing to pay the price.

Two disciples wanted to share glory with Jesus. Jesus was the coolest person they had ever met, and they wanted to be with him in glory. But would they pay the price, drink the cup, walk the walk? What's the cup Jesus is asking if you can drink with him or for him?

## "WHAT DO YOU WANT ME TO DO FOR YOU?"

### MATT. 20:32

I see the homeless more and more. They sit on the ground with cups in front of them, dirty and ragged. Sometimes I plunk a few coins in, but often I keep on moving. In France the homeless are sometimes lame and horribly disfigured, and they display their mangled limbs to get attention and contributions. It's pathetic to see.

Two blind guys were crying out for mercy and heard Jesus was coming. They cried loudly to Jesus saying, "Lord, Son of David, have mercy on us." They did this for years just to survive. But before Jesus did a thing, he asked them what they wanted him to do for them. Put a name to your need, your want. Is it money, food, clothing, shelter, what?

Put a name to what you want Jesus to do for you.

### "JOHN'S BAPTISM—WHERE DID IT COME FROM? WAS IT FROM HEAVEN, OR OF HUMAN ORIGIN?"

*MATT. 21:25*

Jesus won't proof-text. Proof-texting is the tactic of taking a passage of scripture out of context and using it for predesigned purposes: to prove a particular point or to attack an opponent. Jesus stands within the entirety of Scripture as the fulfillment of all of God's promises. John the Baptist was one of those links from prophet to Messiah. And a big component of John the Baptist's ministry was the call to repentance and a conviction of sin. What do you do with John the Baptist? How does he figure as a link between the Old Testament and the New Testament? How authoritatively do you take his words?

"WHAT DO YOU THINK? THERE WAS A MAN WHO HAD TWO SONS. HE WENT TO THE FIRST AND SAID, 'SON, GO AND WORK TODAY IN THE VINEYARD.' 'I WILL NOT,' HE ANSWERED, BUT LATER HE CHANGED HIS MIND AND WENT. THEN THE FATHER WENT TO THE OTHER SON AND SAID THE SAME THING. HE ANSWERED 'I WILL, SIR,' BUT DID NOT GO. WHICH OF THE TWO DID WHAT HIS FATHER WANTED?"

*MATT. 21:28-31*

Jesus likes repentants more than liars. The overtly rebellious son had a change of heart, while the other son said what he knew the father wanted to hear but went and did what he wanted to do instead.

In evangelical circles, there is a lot of emphasis on *praying the prayer* and *saying the words, having a testimony.* We have become so word-centric, so verbal, it almost doesn't matter what we do as opposed to what we say. Do your words match up to your actions, or do your actions outstrip your words? Which son looks and sounds the most like you?

"THEREFORE, WHEN THE OWNER OF THE VINEYARD

COMES, WHAT WILL HE DO TO THOSE TENANTS?"

*MATT. 21:40*

The question Jesus asked here follows a story about abused grace. A vineyard owner wants the rent he is due. He sends a series of servants to collect, and they are abused. He sends his best representative, his son. However, the rebellious tenants, who stupidly think that, if the son is dead, they will inherit the vineyard, end up killing him. How flawed is their logic?

Where do you see God's grace and patience abused today? How have you abused God's grace?

**"YOU HYPOCRITES, WHY ARE YOU TRYING TO TRAP ME?...
WHOSE IMAGE IS THIS? AND WHOSE INSCRIPTION?"**

*MATT. 22:18-20*

Have you ever sensed a trap? Maybe it was at the end of a meeting when someone wanted to *add one more thing* to the agenda, or a person asked you into their office and then asked if you would *close the door, will you?* We sense those moments when the atmosphere changes from collegial to adversarial.

Why would the authorities want to try to *trap* Jesus? What does trapping do? What does trapping someone imply? What has happened to a relationship when we resort to trapping another person? How did Jesus avoid being trapped? How can we?

## "WHAT DO YOU THINK ABOUT THE MESSIAH?
## WHO SON IS HE?"

*MATT. 22:42*

This was not a trick question. Jesus did not ask this question to trap or trip his adversaries. I think he really wanted to know about their hopes for the Messiah and his origin. The promise of the Messiah was and is central to Jewish belief. Where does he come from, and whose son is he? Is he human or divine? Reflect today on Messiah: liberator, rescuer, and savior of the world. What do you think about him?

**"How is it then that David, speaking by the Spirit, calls him 'Lord'? If then David calls him 'Lord,' how can he be his son?"**
*Matt. 22:43-45 (Luke 20:41-44)*

I've never met an angel. I've never seen a ghost. All I meet are humans and animals. I've met some impressive speakers and thinkers and even really, super spiritual people. But they've all been people with mothers and fathers and genetics and DNA. Jesus is different. He's the Son of God with a human mother. That's a brain-stretch.

This question plants the idea that even David knew that the Messiah would not be of his human legacy, but Lord. How does Jesus act as Lord to you?

## "Do you see all these things?"

### Matt. 24:2

As I write this, I'm in France (again), where I am really impressed with old stones. I've seen the Roman Aqueduct called the Pont du Gard, the arenas of Nimes and Arles. I wander obsessively Romanesque churches (10th century and earlier) and get weird over prehistoric "Menhirs," "Dolmens," and cave paintings. I'm impressed by things that last more than a century or two.

In Jesus' day there was no more impressive architecture than the Jerusalem Temple. It was destroyed and rebuilt twice. This was the third edition of the Temple. It was massive and solid. It symbolized everything Israel stood for. There is no modern equivalent for us today. And Jesus asked if they *saw* all these things in and around the Temple? It will not last.

What impressive things have you seen that did not last?

## "WHY ARE YOU BOTHERING THIS WOMAN?"

### MATT. 26:10

When I went to a fragrance store in France to buy new cologne, the salesperson asked if I wanted a sample of what I had bought. I said yes, and she proceeded to spray an aerosol container of the cologne all over my head, hair and jacket. It covered me and drenched me. Wherever I went with that jacket for the next weeks, that particular aroma wafted in the air around me. It was a bit over-the-top for me!

At a dinner a woman, not a salesperson, did the same and more to Jesus—pouring a heavily scented perfume all over him from the head down. This was not normal; it was not part of the decorum of an evening meal with Jesus. It was way, way over-the-top. It was inappropriate, insensitive, maybe even too sensual and tactile for some of the disciples. They objected powerfully to her act, and Jesus objected to them. Why are you bothering her?

Whose devotion to Jesus bothers you? Who might you be bothering?

## "COULDN'T YOU KEEP WATCH WITH ME FOR ONE HOUR?"
### MATT. 26:40 (MARK 14:6)

One hour is really not much time. I've spent hours and hours in airports, in airplanes, in emergency rooms, in surgery waiting rooms, and in committee meetings. What Jesus asked was not that difficult. What happened? It was night; the day had been long; they were tired; and Jesus wanted company as he prayed. It wasn't like he asked them to pray along with him, to pray out loud, or to pray for him; he merely asked them to keep watch, to hang around. Jesus' agenda for his disciples was two-fold: presence and alertness. Where are you present and alert today?

**"ARE YOU STILL SLEEPING AND RESTING?"**
*MATT. 26:45 (MARK 14:41, LUKE 22:46)*

When I first wake up in the morning, that's it, no more sleep for me. I've always been that way. Even when I have the time and want to sleep in, I can't. My mind wakes up the rest of my body. But I have family and friends who love to sleep in. I know people who are so chronically tired that they take multiple naps a day. Sleep is where they go to escape. Sleep is what they do to avoid others. Sleep is where they hide.

How is sleep your friend or your enemy? When are you spiritually asleep, and when are you spiritually awake?

"**Do you think I cannot call on my Father, and he will at once put at my disposal more than twelve legions of angels? But how then would the Scriptures be fulfilled that say it must happen this way?**"

*Matt 26:53, 54*

Jesus' arrest in the garden was filled with tension and spontaneous violence by his own disciples, one who swung a sword and cut off a young man's ear. Jesus did not need their protection or violence. He both saw the bigger picture and was aware of his deeper resources from his father: angels. And he chose not to draw on either but to let the story play out. What does it mean that Jesus let it *happen this way?*

"AM I LEADING A REBELLION, THAT YOU HAVE COME

OUT WITH SWORDS AND CLUBS TO CAPTURE ME?"

*MATT. 26:55 (MARK 14:48, LUKE 22:52, 53)*

The lies about Jesus triggered a mob reaction. He was alleged to be dangerous, seditious, and rebellious to Jewish authorities, laws, and traditions. He was alleged to have plots to destroy the Temple and reject paying taxes to Rome. It's amazing how unfounded rumors can grow and create responses way out of proportion to reality.

What was Jesus leading? Was it a rebellion? What name would you give to what Jesus was leading at the time of his arrest?

## "WHICH IS LAWFUL ON THE SABBATH: TO DO GOOD OR TO DO EVIL, TO SAVE LIFE OR TO KILL?"
### MARK 3:4 (LUKE 6:9, 14:3)

What is lawful on the Sabbath is such a weird question for most of us today. We don't have any Sabbath laws. We do whatever we want to do on the Sabbath. Some of us don't even have or practice a Sabbath. Sabbath is Sunday, and it's part of our weekend. It's a day off, a time to sleep in, go to church if we feel like it, maybe have brunch with friends, or see a movie.

How do we know what is lawful on the Sabbath? What is God's intention for our Sabbath today? What's right and what's wrong to do on the Sabbath?

## "How can Satan drive out Satan?"

### Mark 3:23

Jesus was familiar with evil. Jesus recognized demons and they recognized him. He called them by name and sent them into pigs. It bothered the religious leaders that he was almost comfortable around demons. Therefore, he must be in league with them, they charged—except that Jesus continuously sent them out of people and freed people from their grip. The operative verb in this question is *drive out*. Where is evil being driven out today around you? Where are you helping God drive out Satan?

## "Don't you understand this parable? How then will you understand any parable?"

### *Mark 4:13*

I like the Gospel of Mark because in it the disciples are so dense. They constantly misread Jesus and don't get what he teaches them. Why do I like that? Because the disciples are so much like me. There is hope for me, if there is hope for them. Jesus had just finished telling the parable of the four seeds in the four soils, and they wanted an explanation and a detailed outline and application guide.

I've preached this parable multiple times in my life, and yet Jesus' question is haunting to me: *do I understand this parable? Do I understand any parable?* What does it take for us to really understand a parable as Jesus intends for us to understand? How will you know when you understand a parable?

**"DO YOU BRING IN A LAMP TO PUT IT UNDER A BOWL OR**

**A BED? INSTEAD, DON'T YOU PUT IT ON ITS STAND?"**

*MARK 4:21*

The Bughatti Veyron is an exotic car that costs over a million dollars. It's a car only for the rich and foolish. There is a man in our community who owns one of these exotic cars, but it never leaves his garage. It is so precious, and he is so worried about it being hurt or damaged, that he does not drive it. Isn't that the purpose of a car—to be driven? I know of people who collect fine jewels, art, and wine, who never wear, show or drink the things they collect. Is that wise or foolish?

Isn't that what happens to us when we know the good news of Jesus and keep it to ourselves?

**"WHAT SHALL WE SAY THE KINGDOM OF GOD IS LIKE, OR**

**WHAT PARABLE SHALL WE USE TO DESCRIBE IT?"**

*MARK 4:30 (LUKE 13:18, 20)*

Choose your favorite parable. Choose the parable that best describes the kingdom of God Jesus, which brings to your life. Jesus asked this question and then told the parable of the mustard seed. But he could have chosen any number of his parables. Which one(s) tell your story?

**"WHY ARE YOU SO AFRAID? DO YOU STILL HAVE NO FAITH?"**

*MARK 4:40*

I know what makes me really afraid: fire. In our part of California, we are susceptible to forest fires driven by high winds. These fires race through the land at over 70 mph. When they flare up, all you can do is run. I was never afraid of lightening and thunder, snowstorms, or even tornadoes. But fire terrifies me like nothing ever has before.

Profound fear forces us to look for how our faith does or does not fit in. Sunny weather faith, without fear, is pretty easy. But when the fear settles in the pit of your stomach, and you find it hard to breathe, then is when Jesus asks us, *do you trust me even now?*

### "WHAT IS YOUR NAME?"

*MARK 5:9 (LUKE 8:30)*

As a young boy, I learned that it is not polite to stare or point fingers. My parents were strict about good manners and not asking bold questions like: *why does your foot limp?* Or *what happened to your eye?* And that continues in my life today. I converse more in polite euphemisms rather than stark facts. I talk about *troubles* and *problems, difficulties,* and—my favorite one—*issues. She has some issues* is code language for *she's crazy!*

Jesus had no such compunction about being direct. He named names and called things as they were. In fact, he asked demons to name themselves to him. In my imagination, I wonder how many times he asked the demon(s) this question before getting a straight answer. What's the name (or names) of your *issue?*

### "WHO TOUCHED MY CLOTHES? WHO TOUCHED ME?"

### MARK 5:30, 31 (LUKE 8:45)

Jesus touched many people, but only a few people touched him back. Oh, I'm sure he shook hands and was bumped into, but think of the people in the New Testament who touched him: the woman at the banquet with perfume, this woman, the chief priest's slap, the soldiers' flogging and torturing, Joseph of Arimathea and the women with his dead body, and Thomas.

Why did Jesus want to know who touched him in this crowd? What did it matter? Why did he want this woman to come forward to him? What was he looking for in her?

**"WHY ALL THIS COMMOTION AND WAILING? THE CHILD IS NOT DEAD BUT ASLEEP."**

*MARK 5:39*

There are no funerals more painful than those of children. I have officiated at all sorts of funerals, but when children die, the pain is so thick you can cut through it with a knife. It's deep and wordless grief of lost hope and shattered promise. It's the grief of profound unfairness and victimization.

Jesus has just told Jairus that he would heal his daughter, and all Jairus needed to do was believe in Jesus He was doing just that until they encountered the wailing crowd. There was no hope in the crowd of friends and families, just raw grief and pain. Jesus asked them to suspend their grief because he was at work in this. Can we suspend our wailing and let Jesus go to work at our points of deepest pain?

## "HOW MANY LOAVES DO YOU HAVE? GO AND SEE."

### MARK 6:37

It won't work. It will cost too much money. We don't have nearly enough time. It's too complex of a project for us to undertake. We aren't strong enough or talented enough to pull it off. We've never done anything like this before—ever! It won't work!

Familiar? These are human responses to overwhelming needs. We back down and want to run away. Jesus expects differently from the disciples and from us. He wants us to work for him and for him to work through us. But the first step is willing obedience to go and see *how many do you have?* Moses objected, Jeremiah objected, Jonah certainly objected—until they let God work through them. What do you have today? Go and see.

**"ARE YOU STILL SO DULL? DON'T YOU SEE THAT NOTHING THAT
ENTERS YOU FROM THE OUTSIDE CAN DEFILE YOU?"**

*MARK 7:18*

My father loved to sharpen knives. He had a favorite whetstone that he would moisten and carefully rub the knife blade in circular patterns and then reverse the angle. Back and forth he went, patiently sharpening the knife. Then he would clean the blade and demonstrate its sharpness, often by slicing through a piece of paper silently. Nothing bothered my dad like dull blades on knives, lawn mowers, axes, or saws. Dull does nothing but flail away, leaving a mess.

What is a dull disciple? What does dull faith look like? How do you know if your faith is dull or sharp?

### "HOW MANY LOAVES DO YOU HAVE?"

*MARK 8:5*

I'm sure it's not enough. We don't have sufficient resources to get the job done. It's too expensive. They want too much. I don't have the time that they want from me. I've got too much on my plate.

These are some of the many responses I have when I encounter great need. I doubt. I hesitate. I balk. I am sure that what God asks me to do is basically unrealistic. I don't have what it takes to get the job done. Then the question comes: *what do you have?* Is it that I don't have enough, or is it that what I have I don't really want to release to God for his use?

## "WHY DOES THIS GENERATION ASK FOR A SIGN?"

### MARK 8:12

Prove it! Show me! Put your money where your mouth is! Who do we not suspect anymore? After years and years of scandals, we mistrust politicians, business leaders, physicians, attorneys, the clergy, and the police (to name just a few). Words and promises don't work anymore. We want verifiable proof. "Show me the metrics!" we demand.

How many people in the New Testament do you know about who came to faith by observing a miracle? How effective are miracles and signs in creating genuine faith? Isn't the result of a sign a hunger for another sign, only bigger and better?

"WHY ARE YOU TALKING ABOUT HAVING NO BREAD? DO YOU STILL NOT SEE OR UNDERSTAND? ARE YOU HEARTS HARDENED? DO YOU HAVE EYES BUT FAIL TO SEE, AND EARS BUT FAITH TO HEAR? AND DON'T YOU REMEMBER? WHEN I BROKE THE FIVE LOAVES FOR THE FIVE THOUSAND PEOPLE, HOW MANY BASKETFULS OF PIECES DID YOU PICK UP?"

*MARK 8:17-20*

*Don't you remember* is a question that cuts to the heart. When a child asks a parent to come to an event or to pick them up, and they forget, *don't you remember* hurts. When an anniversary slides by without recognition, especially by a spouse, *don't you remember* aches. When birthdays pass by among family members, and there is no card or phone call *don't you remember* stings.

*Remembering*, in the Bible, is the antidote to sin. Forgetting is the prelude to faithlessness. In stillness today ask God to remind you what he wants you to remember.

## "DO YOU STILL NOT UNDERSTAND?"

### *MARK 8:21*

When the disciples accurately recounted the facts about his miracle of the loaves and fish, Jesus asked this question. Because it's not really about accurately getting all the facts straight, is it? Faith is not about accuracy but something more. Faith is more than parroting back data. Faith needs an "Aha!" Faith needs a heart perception and a willingness to move ahead in trust.

In what faith areas might Jesus be wondering if you still do not understand: about forgiveness, about money, about sex, about anger, about jealousy, about what?

## "WHAT ARE YOU ARGUING WITH THEM ABOUT?"
### MARK 9:16

A crowd is arguing with the disciples about a failed healing. They tried to cast out a demon from a boy, and it did not work (it may have even made his condition worse, but that's just my imagination). The crowd was blaming the disciples for a failure, and the disciples were arguing back. I hate admitting my failures! I don't like my mistakes being found out and made public. I want to blame someone else or find a reason why it's not really my fault.

Note who answered Jesus' question; it was not the disciples, but the father of the demon-possessed boy. Failures are not fatal with Jesus. Our mistakes are stepping-stones to deeper learning. Who will step forward to tell Jesus what your argument is all about?

## "HOW LONG SHALL I STAY WITH YOU? HOW LONG SHALL I PUT UP WITH YOU?"

### MARK 9:19

What do you put up with? I put up with mosquitoes, taxes, traffic, lines, fabric stores, and country music (I know some of you will disagree with a couple of these!). We *put up with* those things we do not want to have surrounding us or occupying our time. Putting up with something is the same as enduring and suffering. Putting up with has no joy or fulfillment about it. It seems to be a waste of time and energy, and we can't wait for it to end.

What does it mean if Jesus admits to having to *put up with* his disciples? What's going on that makes a group that he personally chose become so unpleasant? In what ways does Jesus put up with you?

**"HOW LONG HAS HE BEEN LIKE THIS?"**

*MARK 9:21*

*How long* is a revealing question. *How long* have you had this rash, been in your position of leadership, been unhappy in your marriage, kept this secret, been praying for this person, been following Jesus? *How long* shows the road we've been traveling and how far we have gone. It shows depth or shallowness. It shows deep patience and strength and exhaustion and weariness. What *how long* does God want to know from you today?

## "WHAT WERE YOU ARGUING ABOUT ON THE ROAD?"

### MARK 9:33

An architect friend of mine once told me how he hated designing office spaces. When I asked him why, he said that no area in his business life got more petty than dealing with an office group about who got which space. He told me that people would argue about similar spaces down to the square inches. That scrambling happens throughout our culture, from academic processions and titles to table seating at social events. We incessantly scramble for success, achievement, and just a little bit more than you have!

The disciples were scrambling for the title *greatest*. Who could be considered the greatest and best disciple ever? Most miracles? Most time alone with Jesus? Trusted with the most power? Seating arrangement? Sequence of calling as a disciple? Where does scrambling get in your way of going to the end of the line and being a servant?

**"SALT IS GOOD, BUT IF IT LOSES ITS SALTINESS,
HOW CAN YOU MAKE IT SALTY AGAIN?"**
*MARK 9:50 (LUKE 14:34)*

Is this a trick question? Can salt actually lose its saltiness? Is it still salt if it's not salty? What's Jesus getting at with this question? Salt is good only so far as it interacts with its environment-- to melt, to season, to absorb moisture and preserve, or to intensify a fire. If salt is not used, it's worthless. If someone refuses to be used by Jesus, what does that mean?

## "What did Moses command you?"

### Mark 10:3

Divorce remains a hot-button topic. There is no person I know who has not experienced the pain of divorce by being divorced, having family members go through a divorce, or seeing good friends go through a divorce. The pain of divorce has surely touched everyone reading this. There are no good and sweet divorces. Every divorce is painful, even if it is inevitable and the best choice, it always has hurt around it. Divorce is failure of love and incomplete commitment.

Assigning blame to a divorce is both ineffective and foolish. When Jesus was being set up with this question about divorce, he asked the leaders to go back to scripture and tell him what they read and understood. What does your reading of scripture tell you about both divorce and marriage?

### "WHAT DO YOU WANT ME TO DO FOR YOU?"
*MARK 10:36, 51*

This identical question was asked of both the disciples and blind Bartimaeus. Jesus wants people to be explicit with him. What are they looking for in him? What do they want him to do for them? It implies both a relationship and a power. Jesus wants people to participate in their relationship with him and not be just passive recipients. What explicitly do you want Jesus to do for you today?

## "CAN YOU DRINK THE CUP I DRINK OR BE BAPTIZED WITH THE BAPTISM I AM BAPTIZED WITH?"
### MARK 10:38

What is the cup and baptism Jesus is speaking about? Clearly it is his suffering and death. *Can* is an interesting word. It implies both willingness and ability. It requires a self-knowledge about one's capacities. What can you do for Jesus? How far can you go with Jesus?

## "ARE YOU NOT IN ERROR BECAUSE YOU DO NOT KNOW THE SCRIPTURES OF THE POWER OF GOD?"

*MARK 12:24*

Jesus has just been asked about both resurrection and what happens to married people in the afterlife. Again, it was a trick question. Jesus did not take the bait. His question is two-pronged; it is about scripture and the power of God. His attackers used their own tradition and human arguments to undercut Jesus' teachings. On the surface it seems powerful. Underneath, however, it shows their shallow grasp of the entirety of scripture and a lack of a personal awareness of what God can actually do.

How many times are our errors caught up in this same insufficiency: not knowing the whole bible story and also not knowing the working power of God?

## "WHY DO THE TEACHERS OF THE LAW SAY THAT
## THE MESSIAH IS THE SON OF DAVID?"

*MARK 12:35*

Anthropomorphism is a problem for all of us. Since we're human, we assign human qualities to all sorts of things around us: animal, plants, buildings, and ships. We designate them "him" or "her" and give them names and talk to them. But most of all, we make God human. Maybe it's the highest praise we can give God, to make him like us.

The Jews also took the prophecies for the Messiah and made them human. They made the Messiah into a human heir of King David. That meant the Messiah was like them and was one of them. And that meant the Messiah served the needs of their particular community. Jesus pushed back. The Messiah is more than for Israel, more than for America, more than for the Christian church. The Messiah is for the entire world. Where does your view of the Messiah need to be expanded?

**"DO YOU SEE ALL THESE GREAT BUILDINGS?"**

*MARK 13:2*

Great architecture impresses me: Notre Dame cathedral in Paris, the Millau Viaduct in France, the Sears Tower in Chicago, the Golden Gate bridge in San Francisco, the Disney Music Hall in Los Angeles. I am impressed when great buildings soar and pierce the sky with their beauty. Jesus too saw the beauty and impressiveness of the Temple in Jerusalem. It was magnificent architecture, full of symbolism and heritage. He wanted his disciples to see and appreciate it too. But there is more than great buildings and impressive architecture. What buildings do you see and take note of? What does that mean?

## "SIMON, ARE YOU ASLEEP? COULD YOU NOT KEEP WATCH FOR ONE HOUR?"

### MARK 14:37

*Are you asleep* is an impossible question to answer. If I answer it, I'm clearly not asleep. If I'm asleep, I won't hear the question. How do you know if you are asleep or awake? How do you know if you are spiritually asleep or awake? Ask God to wake you up today in new and alert ways.

"**WHY ARE YOU THINKING THESE THINGS IN YOUR HEARTS? WHICH IS EASIER; TO SAY 'YOUR SINS ARE FORGIVEN,' OR TO SAY 'GET UP AND WALK?'**"

*LUKE 5:22,23*

This question can twist. It can be read, *which is easier?* or *which is easier to say?* On the one hand, is it easier to make someone stand up or to make their sins go away and receive forgiveness? On the other hand, which words are easier to say, something interior that can neither be proved nor disproved, like forgiveness of sins, or something evident and obvious to all, like *stand up and walk*? Is this question about saying or doing? What is the connection between the words you say and the deeds you do?

**"CAN YOU MAKE THE FRIENDS OF THE BRIDEGROOM**

**FAST WHILE HE IS WITH THEM?"**

*LUKE 5:34*

Have you noticed how different cultures eat? Some consider eating like a pit stop in an auto race—something to be done as quickly and efficiently as possible. Other cultures see meals as times to slowly celebrate each course and every flavor, stopping between courses to talk and enjoy both the food and the company. On the continuum from fast to slow, where do you put yourself in eating speed? How well do you linger in celebration, or how fast do you need to get back to serious business? What would it look like today if you celebrated and enjoyed Jesus for his own sake?

"CAN THE BLIND LEAD THE BLIND? WILL THEY NOT
BOTH FALL INTO A PIT?"

*LUKE 6:39*

I once saw a blind skier at a ski area. It was an amazing sight! He skied all by himself down a slope, while a guide skied directly behind him with a whistle. The guide would make unique whistle sounds indicating which direction the blind skier should turn to avoid the trees. It really worked.

But the reverse would be disastrous. If the blind skier had the whistle, he would certainly head into the trees and crash. Who do you allow to lead you? Who do you allow to give directions to your life? What do they see? How sighted are they?

**"WHY DO YOU CALL ME, 'LORD, LORD,'
AND DO NOT DO WHAT I SAY?"**
*LUKE 6:46*

I'm no longer impressed with churchy talk. I've been in the church for too many years to be fooled by someone with great and flowery words. I've even grown to dislike "preacher talk." You know what I mean. It's when a preacher's voice modulates into a deeply resonant tone, dripping with religion. It bellows and warbles like an actor putting on a different character than whom he or she is. It's not the talk; it's the walk that matters to Jesus.

What is it that he is asking you to do? What next steps are Jesus' words asking you to take for him?

**"TO WHAT THEN CAN I COMPARE THE PEOPLE OF
THIS GENERATION? WHAT ARE THEY LIKE?"**

*LUKE 7:31, 32*

Jesus knew his audience. Jesus knew his sociology. He had his finger on the pulse of his community and culture. And he was not impressed. He cared and loved people, but he was not fooled by them. How well do you know *this generation* in which you live? Which words and terms would you use to describe your current community? Jesus answer to his question was *children*. This generation is like children, always wanting to be entertained. What's your word?

"TWO PEOPLE OWED MONEY TO A CERTAIN MONEYLENDER. ONE OWED HIM FIVE HUNDRED DENARII, AND THE OTHER FIFTY. NEITHER OF THEM HAD THE MONEY TO PAY HIM BACK, SO HE FORGAVE THE DEBTS OF BOTH. NOW WHICH OF THEM WILL LOVE HIM MORE?"

*LUKE 7:41,42*

I've owed people money many times in my life, and I have always paid back people what I owed them, even if it took years. Many years ago, I received notice that I owed back-taxes to the government in an amount I could not pay. I was deeply distressed and went to some wise advisors for help. And while they sent me to tax accountants to find a possible solution, I still owed a large amount of money in a short period of time. One man told me that he would lend me the full amount I owed. I had no choice but to accept it and make a schedule to pay him back over time. When the time came for my first payment he said, "I've decided to forgive the loan. Consider it a gift!"

I will always love that man for what he did for me. I fully intended to pay him back, but he forgave a very large debt I owed him. Now I will always hold him closely in my heart. Who has forgiven you a great debt?

## "Do you see this woman?"

*Luke 7:44*

I live in a community of wealthy people who have household staff and host large parties. When I've attended the parties, those who serve the meals are meant to be invisible. They seldom speak but silently and graciously clear dirty plates and refill beverages. I've grown accustomed to attending these events and pay attention to the hosts. My dilemma comes when one of the "servants" is a friend of mine: a student from the local college who attends church or someone I've met in other circumstances. I've chosen to *see* them and spend time talking with them, though they are sometimes uncomfortable stepping out of their working role to talk with me as an equal.

But I've learned, painfully, that I am part of the "service-sector" in our community as well. I live in a house provided by the church for the current pastor. When I stop being pastor, I must leave my house. I live a subsidized life as a servant among servants. Who lives invisibly around you that God wants you to see? Who are the "service-sector" people who live all-but-invisibly around you?

**"WHERE IS YOUR FAITH?"**

*LUKE 8:25*

I love the smart-phone's ability to act as a GPS. I love how I can hit a button, and a map shows up with a blue flag showing me exactly where I am right now. I like those apps that can show me where friends of mine are with their phones right now.

But how do you locate your faith? What language do you use to answer Jesus' question above about *where is your faith*? Is it a developmental answer, a geographical answer, a historical answer, a relational answer? Where is the blue flag that represents your faith today?

## "WHAT IS WRITTEN IN THE LAW? HOW DO YOU READ IT?"

### *LUKE 10:26*

*What* and *how* are two different questions. One requires the other. The *how* requires knowing the *what*. I remain amazed at people's contentment at being Biblically illiterate—even ignorant. I am shocked at how few believers I know regularly read the Bible alone. I am dismayed at how few people bring their Bibles to church with them and read along with me and engage the word personally. Rather, they opt for a mediated faith, a faith that comes in pre-digested pieces—outlined, alliterated, and even illustrated with a video clip. How do you know what is written in the Law? When was the last time you leisurely read through the five books of the Law? Is it time again?

## "WHICH OF THESE THREE DO YOU THINK WAS A NEIGHBOR TO THE MAN WHO FELL INTO THE HANDS OF ROBBERS?"

### *LUKE 10:36*

This question follows the familiar parable of the Good Samaritan. It involves three archetypical people on the road to Jericho (a dangerous road way out in the wilderness, even today!). The three men were a Priest, a Levite, and a Samaritan. In Jesus' class-divided day, there were lines one never crossed. It just wasn't done. Nobody would blame you for staying within your social class boundary. But we do not know which class "the man" belonged to, who fell victim to robbers. He was just a man, a human, a person. A neighbor then (and now) was someone within your community, someone within your class. Today we call it zip codes.

Jesus hates class divisions, boundaries, and walls. He rejects those distinctions that keep us away from each other and give us permission to ignore another person. Neighbor is defined by need, compassion, and mercy. Who comes to mind as your neighbor today?

**"WHICH OF YOU FATHERS, IF YOUR SON ASKS FOR A FISH, WILL GIVE HIM A SNAKE INSTEAD? OR IF HE ASKS FOR AN EGG, WILL GIVE HIM A SCORPION?"**

*LUKE 11:11*

I don't know many bad fathers. I know several men who are good dads but jerks to other people. I know some guys with bad tempers and overindulged egos, but when it comes to their kids, they really try to do right by them. It's a "dad" thing. I want my kids to say at my grave, "He was a good dad." That's all.

Jesus gets that. He observed his earthly dad, Joseph, and other dads around him. He saw how dads tried to do right by their kids whether they were rich or poor. Dads live to give to their children, and they try to give their children good things. And guess what? All of us dads are sinners!

But there is a perfect Father, a perfect parent…God. He will only give us what is best for us. Ask him for what you need today.

**"You foolish people! Did not the one who makes the outside make the inside also?"**

*Luke 11:40*

Oops! He slipped up and forgot to wash his hands, not hygienically but ceremonially. That was a big "no, no" among the Pharisees in Jesus' day. Who knows where your hands have been and what (or whom) they have touched. Clearly this was a "gotcha" moment for the leaders to point out Jesus' failure as a religious leader. It would be as if a driving instructor forgot to fasten his/her seatbelt!

I can be just as critical about other believers. I can criticize poor wardrobe choices, unkempt hair, improper manners, or bad grammar. It's amazing the faults I can see in others' outside appearance. What are some of the *foolish* things that distract you?

## "MAN, WHO APPOINTED ME A JUDGE OR AN ARBITER BETWEEN YOU?"

### *LUKE 12:14*

Police say there are few more dangerous calls than a domestic dispute between relatives or married couples. Long-simmering anger can erupt into catastrophic violence because of intense relationships. Jesus was asked to get involved in a domestic dispute about inheritance and money. And he would not bite.

Where have you been hooked or triangled into a domestic dispute? What family conflicts have drawn you in? Who appointed you as judge (unless you are a judge reading this!)?

"**But God said to him, 'You fool! This very night your life will be demanded from you. Then who will get what you have prepared for yourself?'**"

*Luke 12:20*

The conclusion of the parable of the rich man ends with a question. The rich man had success upon success. Since he had acquired so much grain that he could no longer store it, he built more storage and decided to retire, to take it easy after a life of hard work and success. What's wrong with that? Isn't this part of the dream we all have? Don't we all hope to have sufficient or abundant resources after a life of hard work to be able to sit back, put our feet up and relax? Where is this guy's sin? Why does God call him a fool? Where is the error in his strategy?

It seems that the energy of this question sits with the phrase *who will get* in the last sentence. The answer would be his heirs. That is who gets all his wealth—his earthly heirs. Nothing goes with us after death. The deeper dimension of this question is how do we get real wealth toward God?

"WHO THEN IS THE FAITHFUL AND WISE MANAGER, WHOM THE
MASTER PUTS IN CHARGE OF HIS SERVANTS AND TO GIVE THEM
THEIR FOOD ALLOWANCE AT THE PROPER TIME?"

*LUKE 12:42*

This is part of a series of parables Jesus told, which focused
on the need to be prepared and to be a good steward of what has
been entrusted to us. What is entrusted and what's mine? What
belongs to another person and is in my care temporarily, and
what is mine to do with as I please? Where do you draw the line
between ownership and stewardship?

I formerly owned two homes in cities where I served churches.
The churches helped us purchase homes, but they were our
homes. I could paint, nail, and make repairs any way I chose. I
did not need to consult with any committee for permission. Now
I am back in a church-owned home, a parsonage that is clearly
not mine. Funds for repairs come out of a church budget and
need approval before being spent. Now I am clearly a steward of
what is not mine. Where are you a steward?

## "DO YOU THINK I CAME TO BRING PEACE ON EARTH?"

### *LUKE 12:51*

Jesus is not Disneyland. Jesus' message of salvation does not always create applause and conjure warm feelings. To make things right, the wrong needs to be brought to light. To bring peace, war needs to be renounced. To bring love, hate needs to be stamped out. In what ways has Jesus' message surprised and even disappointed you?

"HOW IS IT THAT YOU DON'T KNOW HOW TO INTERPRET
THE TIME? WHY DON'T YOU JUDGE FOR YOURSELVES
WHAT IS RIGHT?"
*LUKE 12:56,57*

As I write this from France, my family is back in the United States in three different time zones. When it is morning here, the day is ending back home. When it is mid-afternoon, it is past midnight there. We have learned to "time" our calls. We know what time it is here and there. Knowing the time is an important life skill in many ways. Being punctual is practicing good manners. Meeting deadlines is good business. Remembering birthdays is good for family life.

What are some of the ways you interpret time? Where does time fit in your spiritual rhythm and cadence? When have you not gotten it right? What time is it in your walk with God?

> **"DO YOU THINK THAT THESE GALILEANS WERE**
> **WORSE SINNERS THAN ALL THE OTHER GALILEANS**
> **BECAUSE THEY SUFFERED IN THIS WAY?"**
> *LUKE 13:2*

We all assign blame. When there are natural disasters, pundits and experts come in for analysis and try to think of both what caused the problem and how or who could have helped avoid it. We look for reasons, and we look for culprits.

In a building disaster in Galilee, rumor had it that it came upon them as God's punishment for some religious reason. Jesus questioned that. Bad stuff happens in a broken world to good and bad people alike. Onto what people group are you prone to assign blame? Are they as bad as you think they are?

## "WHY SHOULD IT USE UP THE SOIL?"

### *LUKE 13:7*

This question comes in the middle of a parable about a fig tree that just would not bear fruit. It was big, shade producing, and full of leaves, but no fruit. The landowner was not interested in making a park, but in producing fruit, and he (the voice of Jesus) asked why it should *use up the soil*. What does it mean to *use up the soil*? It means taking without giving back, consuming without producing.

How many believers are like that barren fig tree? They show up at church, sit through a service and go home again. They put in their time and maybe even contribute some money. But where is the fruit? They consume programs, services, and time but produce few disciples. The question looks even closer at me. Where is my fruit after following Jesus all these years? Am I productive in his eyes or *using up the soil?*

**"Then should not this woman, a daughter of Abraham, whom Satan has kept bound for eighteen long years be set free on the Sabbath day from what bound her?"**

*Luke 13:16*

The words that grab my attention in this question are *set free*. *Set free* is such a wonderful image. It speaks of joy and liberty, life and wonder. It looks like movement and dancing, laughter and singing. According to Jesus, the Sabbath is a great day and a time for freeing what has been bound. How does your Sabbath practice free you from what has bound you?

**"WON'T YOU FIRST SIT DOWN AND ESTIMATE THE COST**

**TO SEE IF YOU HAVE ENOUGH MONEY TO COMPLETE IT?"**

*LUKE 14:28*

There is a curious house in the village where we stay in France. It is up the hill from us on a nice big lot. It is a big house, two full stories with an exterior porch. However, it is bare cinderblock. It's been bare cinderblock for 6 years! It's not finished! Why? What happened in the life of that family that prevented them from finishing a lovely house project?

Unfinished business is a nagging indictment on poor planning or inadequate resources to get a job done. I'm sure all of us have some project stuck away in a closet or basement that was never finished. For some reason we lost the energy to get the job done and now do not want to be reminded of it.

What is spiritually unfinished in your life? Where do you need to sit down again and calculate what it would take to get the job done?

"So if you have not been trustworthy in handling worldly
wealth, who will trust you with true riches? And if you
have not been trustworthy with someone else's property,
who will give you property of your own?"
*Luke 16:11, 12*

I watch people who "rent" the church I serve for weddings, funerals or celebrations. It's amazing how poorly people treat property that is not their own. They leave trashcans filled and countertops dirty. They have even asked me what I was doing on the property that they had "rented for the day," as if I was a trespasser or an interloper.

How do you measure *trustworthiness*? With what have you been entrusted today? Money? Relationships? A task? A business? How would you rank yourself in terms of trustworthiness? Would you lend your stuff to you?

"DOESN'T HE LEAVE THE NINETY-NINE IN THE OPEN
COUNTRY AND GO AFTER THE LOST SHEEP UNTIL HE
FINDS IT? DOESN'T SHE LIGHT A LAMP, SWEEP THE
HOUSE AND SEARCH CAREFULLY UNTIL SHE FINDS IT?"

*LUKE 15:4, 8*

I routinely lose things: keys, glasses, pens, pieces of paper, and remote controls. I set things down somewhere and can't remember where I put them last. And I spend enormous amounts of time and energy searching for and finding lost little things. I often find myself angry about something I own not being where I need it to be. I do not like losing things that belong to me, even if they are small and trivial. I want to retrieve it and bring it back to where it belongs.

Jesus told two stories about a lost sheep and a lost coin. The shepherd and the homeowner each invested their energy to what was lost. They did not blame the lost objects or punish them, but they searched for them to restore them to their rightful place. For what lost thing did you recently search? Who do you know who qualifies for being a lost sheep or a lost coin? Who is no longer around—no longer part of the church—who needs finding?

"SUPPOSE ONE OF YOU HAS A SERVANT PLOWING OR LOOKING
AFTER THE SHEEP. WILL HE SAY TO THE SERVANT WHEN HE
COMES IN FROM THE FIELD, 'COME ALONG NOW AND SIT DOWN
TO EAT?' WON'T HE RATHER SAY, 'PREPARE MY SUPPER, GET
YOURSELF READY AND WAIT ON ME WHILE I EAT AND DRINK; AND
AFTER THAT YOU MAY EAT AND DRINK?'"

*LUKE 17:7-9*

What do you expect? That's what Jesus is getting at in this question. What are your expectations and sense of entitlement? Mine keep growing like weeds. I expect to be appreciated, thanked, liked, listened to, and paid well. I expect success, gratitude, appreciation, and frequent trips to France. I don't expect to submit, suffer, lose, and serve. I see myself as an owner-operator, self-employed, and obligated to no one (other than my family).

Jesus seeks to recalibrate our sense of entitlement: we are called to be disciples, followers, and servants. What does that mean in your world today?

**"WERE NOT ALL TEN CLEANSED? WHERE ARE THE OTHER NINE? WAS NO ONE FOUND TO RETURN AND GIVE PRAISE TO GOD EXCEPT THIS FOREIGNER?"**

*LUKE 17:17, 18*

"Who taught you gratitude?" is another question I ask young couples preparing for marriage. Who taught you how to say, "Thank you"? Sadly, many who sit before me give me a blank stare back. They have no immediate role model for gratitude or generosity. They grew up in a family and community of takers, demanders, and complainers. They neither give nor celebrate. They consume and move on.

Jesus had just healed ten persons from a terminal disease called leprosy. It was so bad that they had to leave their lives and live in isolated communities until they died. No touching of anyone any more. Jesus set them free and sent them home. But only one came back to say thank you…a non-Jew, a foreigner. Who is your model for gratitude? Who taught you to give thanks to God?

> "AND WILL NOT GOD BRING ABOUT JUSTICE FOR
> HIS CHOSEN ONES, WHO CRY OUT TO HIM DAY AND
> NIGHT? WILL HE KEEP PUTTING THEM OFF?"
> *LUKE 18:7*

Is God fair? Is God just? The headlines I read each day don't say so. Tragedy, injustice, and scandal pile up on each other. People are killed, tortured, and taken advantage of all over the world. The poor seem to get poorer, and vulnerable ones suffer horribly. Does God care? Does God bring justice? If so, when? This question slams our beliefs against the wall: will God make things right? What things around you need to be made right again by God?

## "HOWEVER, WHEN THE SON OF MAN COMES, WILL HE FIND FAITH ON THE EARTH?"

### *LUKE 18:8*

I've stopped trying to fix people. That's a hard admission for a pastor to make. For years and years I ran to the rescue of people in trouble with lists of good advice. I had tips and suggestions, practices and attitudes that they should adopt. The harder I tried, the more they resisted. Then I realized that I could not create faith in anyone but me. I can witness, teach, preach, and encourage, but I cannot create faith in another person. That is his/her responsibility.

Where is your faith growing today? Where is your faith being pushed and stretched to its limits? Where does your faith flourish and where is it dry as dust? What would you like God to do with your faith today?

## "WHY DO YOU CALL ME GOOD?"

### *LUKE 18:19*

"I'm *good*," is a quick answer we often give to people, who ask us if we want more food or beverage. "No thanks, I'm *good*" we shoot back. *Good* is a noun and an adjective, and we use so frequently it loses all its meaning: *good* weather, *good* news, *good* afternoon, *good* meal, *good* job, *good* friend, *good* _____?

Why is Jesus *good* in your eyes? What makes him *good* in any way for you?

### "WHAT DO YOU WANT ME TO DO FOR YOU?"

*LUKE 18:41*

I am amazed how Jesus never imposes himself on other people. He listens, observes, asks questions, and responds. The context for this question is the plea of a blind man for Jesus to *have mercy* on him. He is clearly blind and disabled. Duh! Isn't it obvious what Jesus *should* do for this guy? Yet Jesus asked him the question above. *What do you want me to do for you? What impact do you want me to make on your life? How far do you want me to make a dent in your life?*

Imagine yourself meeting Jesus at the front door of your church on a Sunday morning, and he greets you and asks you the very same question: *what do you want me to do for you today?* What real difference do you want Jesus to make in your life right now, today?

## "TELL ME, JOHN'S BAPTISM—WAS IT FROM HEAVEN OR OF HUMAN ORIGIN?"

*LUKE 20:3, 4*

Is there truth beyond Jesus? Can we compartmentalize Jesus' life and words and avoid the prophetic traditions with all their ranting and raving about sin and repentance? Can't we just enjoy the person and work of Jesus and avoid the messiness of the Old Testament with all of its rules and regulations?

Jesus' question to the religious authorities is a question to us as well. How seriously do we take those who came before Jesus in obedient response to God? How much of an impact does the rest of Scripture make on our lives?

**"THEN WHAT IS THE MEANING OF THAT WHICH IS WRITTEN: 'THE STONE THE BUILDERS REJECTED HAS BECOME THE CORNERSTONE'?"**

*LUKE 20:17*

Jesus quotes Psalm 118:22 to the religious leaders who questioned his authority. The entire landscape of Israel is (still today) stone. There are few trees and an overwhelming amount of rocks. Most buildings were and are made of stone (or cement today). A good stonemason knows which stones work for building and which ones don't. Bad stones, stones with flaws and impediments, are tossed into a rubble pile and become landfill.

A cornerstone is so much more than a regular building stone. It is a stone that sets the angle and direction of the entire building. Or, if you choose arch-stone instead of cornerstone, it is the top-most stone in an arch that supports the weight of each side and bears the load of the whole wall.

How does Jesus set the direction of your life and bear the weight of what you endure?

"FOR WHO IS GREATER, THE ONE WHO IS AT THE
TABLE OR THE ONE WHO SERVES? IS IT NOT THE
ONE WHO IS AT THE TABLE?"

*LUKE 22:27*

What are the ways you mark greatness around you: size of houses, corporate title, dollars amassed, success of children, college you attended, circle of friends? We all have our ways of telling who or what is greater than another. A Rolls Royce is greater than a Ford; a diamond is greater than plastic; a penthouse apartment is greater than a tent.

Who is greater than you? Are you greater than others around you? Jesus shatters all our attempts at ranking by calling us to be waitstaff to the world around us, rather than sitting at the head table. Where can you be a waiter today?

## "WHEN I SENT YOU OUT WITHOUT PURSE, BAG OR SANDALS, DID YOU LACK ANYTHING?"

### *LUKE 22:35*

*Enough* is such a shifting word. When is *enough*? When do we have *enough* money in the bank, time to relax, clothes in our closet, or books in our library? If you are like me, I always have this nagging quest for *more...just a little bit more...of everything*. That only serves to supply me with an excuse about why I cannot obey, go, do, or serve. Why? Because I don't have enough training, faith, support, skills, spiritual maturity. I endlessly try to find reasons why I cannot be the one God wants to use because I don't have *enough* _____.

Look back on your faith life. When did God fail you? When was he not adequate? When did you not have *enough?*

## "Judas, are you betraying the Son of Man with a kiss?"
### *Luke 22:48*

People in France greet each other with a kiss on the cheek. It shows what part of France you come from by the number of kisses you give: one, two, three, or four. But generally, kissing is reserved for those you already know and are familiar with. As a foreigner and stranger, I am often greeted the first time with a handshake and then, later, with a kiss. Kissing is special.

What does kissing mean to you? Who is the last person you kissed? Who has recently kissed you? Why would Judas choose a kiss to signal betrayal? What does it mean to use a gesture of intimacy and friendship as an instrument for betrayal? How have good gestures been used to accomplish evil things?

**"FOR IF A PEOPLE DO THESE THINGS WHEN THE
TREE IS GREEN, WHAT HAPPENS WHEN IT IS DRY?"**

*LUKE 23:31*

I can hardly believe this question! Jesus has been arrested, tried, tortured, and is now walking to his crucifixion death with crowds wailing around him. In the verses immediately preceding this question, he urged the wailing women not to weep for him but for themselves and the tough times they would soon be facing.

*These things* surely refers to the authorities crucifying Jesus without cause, for doing good things. People, institutions, authorities, powers, and principalities can act with cruel efficiency in the best of times. But when times get tough (read *dry*), they can turn brutal. Who do you know who has or is experiencing unjust persecution today?

## "WHAT ARE YOU DISCUSSING TOGETHER AS YOU WALK ALONG?"

### LUKE 24:17

Sunday afternoons for pastors can be brutal. Meals with friends or family can quickly devolve into *worship autopsies*. Pastors are the worst at picking apart everything that did not conform to their expectations. The music was too fast or slow, loud or quiet. The testimony was too long. The illustration flopped. The response was meager. And on and on we go, piling disappointment on top of disappointment.

The two men Jesus encountered were doing the same thing, but with much greater intensity. They were analyzing what went wrong with the ministry of Jesus that he had to die like he did. They had such high hopes and were now so deeply disappointed.

I honestly do not really want to go to those places and persons where I feel such deep disappointment. Faces pop up as I write this of people I had such high hopes in who let me down, or worse, betrayed me. Jesus wants in on that discussion—the one about disappointments and failed expectations. Where are you most disappointed today? Will you let Jesus in on that conversation?

## "WHAT THINGS?"

### LUKE 24:19

There are certain words we use that say *stay away*. They are words like: *stuff, you know, so-so, same old, junk,* and *things*. Jesus followed up with the men on the road to Emmaus about their deep, spiritual disappointments. When he came to ask them specifics, they tried to foil him with the word *things*. That's another way of saying *I don't want to talk about it anymore. I'm disappointed and sad; so leave it alone!*

What are the *things* Jesus wants to talk with you about today? Where are those areas you have closed off with the same label the men on the road tried to use?

## "DID NOT THE MESSIAH HAVE TO SUFFER THESE THINGS AND THEN ENTER HIS GLORY?"

### *LUKE 24:26*

I'm amazed at how selectively I still read scripture. I underline and delight in those passages that speak of the fruit of the Spirit, of abiding in Christ, of the peace that passes understanding, of restoration and reconciliation. And I skip quickly over instructions to submit to others, to bear suffering, to experience rejection, to live as a foreigner, and other tough passages.

Jesus called the men on the road, and he calls us to see him in light of all of scripture and not just those passages we like. What are some of the tough places in scripture where God might be speaking to you?

**"WHY ARE YOU TROUBLED, AND WHY DO DOUBTS
ARISE IN YOUR MINDS?"**

*LUKE 24:38*

She was a faithful, older woman from the church. She called me to visit her apartment to pray for her. When I arrived, she told me about a complicated medical condition for which she wanted me to pray for her healing. I pulled out my book of worship, anointed her head with oil, prayed the words of James 5:14-15, and gave her a benediction.

The next Sunday she showed up at church. I asked her how she was and she said, "Completely healed! The doctors confirmed it the next day. The condition reversed itself." I said "Really?" and she quickly responded back, "Of course, pastor, you prayed for it, and God honored it." Things like that do not happen that often and that suddenly with me. And I had to repent later to God how I doubted his healing touch in this woman's life. That's because we get used to life being the normal flow of our experience. And when God intervenes, we often doubt. Where is God asking you to go from doubt to belief?

## "DO YOU HAVE ANYTHING HERE TO EAT?"

### *LUKE 24:41*

I love this question. The resurrected Jesus meets his surprised disciples. This is about as spiritual an experience any person could ever have—to encounter the resurrected Jesus face to face in a room with others. What should they do? Worship, pray, sing, or bow down?

Jesus got real normal with them and said, "Let's *eat!*" And to me he might say, "Have any fresh coffee Don?" Jesus wanted to get back into their normal lives and conversations, and nothing does that more effectively than sharing a meal together. It demands hospitality and service. It demands sharing and generosity. Where could Jesus be asking you to share a meal with someone today?

## "WHAT DO YOU WANT?"

### JOHN 1:38

There are times I want to be left alone just to browse. It's often when I am out shopping with my wife and she enters one type of store (fabric or clothing), and I enter another one (book or hardware). I have no item in mind other than to occupy time until we meet up with each other again. If a clerk comes up to me and asks me if I need any help, I quickly answer, "No, just browsing," and hope they will leave me alone.

But there are other times when I enter a store searching for a particular item. Those are the times when I need help finding what I'm looking for. My body posture and movement indicates that I'm looking for something. But it takes a clerk to help me figure out exactly what it is that I need.

Jesus noticed two of John the Baptist's disciples following him. They said nothing, but followed after Jesus, looking for something. In your movement and following, what is it that you want? What is it that you are looking for?

"WOMAN, WHY DO YOU INVOLVE ME?
MY HOUR HAS NOT YET COME."

*JOHN 2:4*

The first miracle of Jesus in John's Gospel is prompted by his mother. The wedding party was running out of wine, and his mother told Jesus about the need. Is Jesus surprised, perturbed, startled, or eager? Is he asking his mother if she is addressing him as her son or as the Messiah? What is his emerging role with respect to his mother and the community around him? He came to the wedding as an invited guest, and now his role was about to shift. Why do you involve Jesus in your life today? What emerging role do you wish Jesus to play in your affairs?

**"YOU ARE ISRAEL'S TEACHER, AND YOU DO NOT UNDERSTAND THESE THINGS?"**

*JOHN 3:10*

It's all about being born again, or born from above. Jesus and old Nicodemus are having a discussion about spiritual priorities, and Nicodemus just doesn't get it. He's been involved with religion so long that all he can see are the complexities. Religion can do that. It has done that to me as a pastor after many, many years. I can get so involved in budgets, building operations, and administrative details, that I no longer understand the really important things. Details can do that. They can obscure truly important things with petty concerns. What things might you not fully understand today?

"I HAVE SPOKEN TO YOU OF EARTHLY THINGS AND YOU DO
NOT BELIEVE; HOW THEN WILL YOU BELIEVE IF I SPEAK OF
HEAVENLY THINGS?"

*JOHN 3:12*

I have a problem being still and quiet. I like being active and busy. Sitting still and waiting is most difficult for me. I am wrestling with how well or poorly I understand what it means to practice Sabbath rest. If I am unable to fully practice simple Sabbath resting, how can I understand deeper spiritual truths? This extends also into areas like tithing, forgiveness, submission, and suffering. If I have such a hard time with clear and simple spiritual instructions, how can God take me deeper into the mysteries of the Spirit? List and name those spiritual areas and topics you are still having a hard time believing. Offer them up to God as a confession.

## "WILL YOU GIVE ME A DRINK?"

### JOHN 4:7

A banner over the life of Jesus could be titled: *good food with bad people.* Here is a brilliant example of this. Jesus asks for water from a known woman of ill repute. She went through men on a rotating basis. Her life was a moral train wreck. That's why she was at the well during the heat of the day, when no one else would be there to harass her or click their tongues at her. Instead of lecturing her, Jesus asked her for water, for help to ease his thirst. Jesus invited her in to his life with something she could give—a cup of water. Of course, the conversation went deeper and deeper. She offered Jesus water for his physical thirst, and he offered her water for her spiritual thirst.

What simple request could Jesus be asking from you today? What simple gesture on his behalf can you make towards others? What will you give him?

## "DO YOU WANT TO GET WELL?"

### JOHN 5:6

I am amazed at how Jesus approached chronic conditions. This man to whom Jesus asked this question had been sitting by this healing pool for thirty-eight years with no success, with no healing. Every time the waters stirred (indicating a potential healing), someone else jumped in first.

*Do you want to get well?* Is this an insulting question? Why else would he keep coming back every day for thirty-eight years if he did not want to get well? But his response told Jesus that all he could do now was blame; blame others and blame God. He remained sick because others beat him to the waters. Blame is so much easier than healing. Healing requires change and responsibility. Blame permits whining and pity to go on unabated.

Who do you chronically blame? Who are the perpetual excuses for why things are bad around you? Who are the constant targets for your anger and disappointment? *Do you want to get well yet?*

**"HOW CAN YOU BELIEVE SINCE YOU ACCEPT GLORY**

**FROM ONE ANOTHER BUT DO NOT SEEK THE GLORY**

**THAT COMES FROM GOD?"**

*JOHN 5:44*

This is not a complicated question. I love glory from other people (e.g. "Pastor, that was the *best* sermon I've ever heard on that text! He is one of our outstanding senior pastors!") I eat up glory other people give me. I like awards and accolades, thank you letters and even applause. It's visible, tangible, and recognized by others. Glory from God is kind of different, isn't it? It's so interior and spiritual. It neither needs validation from others nor depends upon the votes of other people.

The deeper question within this question is: how do I know that God is giving me glory, and I'm not just talking to myself? How can I be sure it's from God and not from myself? Does God's glory come to us now, or is it an end-of-time sort of thing? What is the connection to God's glory and your worshiping life? How does weekly worship bring you into and help you experience God's glory?

## "WHERE SHALL WE BUY BREAD FOR THESE PEOPLE TO EAT?"

### JOHN 6:5

Jesus invited his disciples into the miracle of feeding the 5,000 people by first inviting them into the problem: *where, buy, bread, these people, eat?* Location, resources, material, target population, and action; these were the steps the disciples were invited to walk through with Jesus before Jesus did anything.

Whose responsibility was the crowd—Jesus' or the disciples'? Who is responsible for the need for food—the crowd itself (they should have made preparations for feeding themselves since they went out to see and hear Jesus!)? I confess that I try to avoid responsibility for large groups of people. I have led tours to the Holy Land and have felt the responsibility for a whole group, and it's seldom fun. The older I get, the more I run from the needs of large groups—until Jesus asks the question. What group comes to your mind when Jesus asks this question to you?

## "DOES THIS OFFEND YOU?"

### JOHN 6:60

Religion is respectable and accepted; Jesus is embarrassingly specific and straightforward. We can work and manipulate religions and traditions to make them swing our way and emphasize what we like (conservative or liberal leanings) and de-emphasize what we do not like. We can focus in on some things and avoid others. Religion is like an all-you-can-eat buffet line, where we can pick and choose.

Not so with Jesus. In this text he gets awkwardly specific about who he is and what he can do...and what we must do with him. Eat him and drink him is weird. It's way too graphic. I prefer *understand* and *accept* over *eat* and *drink* body and blood.

Guess what? Jesus does not care if we are offended or not. Jesus is truth, and truth does not depend upon votes for approval. Where do Jesus' words offend you most? Where do they make you pause and even rub you the wrong way? Lean into those places today and ask God to stretch and open your heart.

## "You do not want to leave too, do you?"

### John 6:67

As a long-term pastor, I know too much. I've gone through too many Easter pageants and Christmas Eve services. People's expectations are high; traditions run deeply, and emotions rule the day. I know some part of the congregation will not be satisfied with some aspect of the worship services. The music will be too contemporary or too traditional, too loud or too soft. We are not doing it the way we have always done it or we are stuck in the boring rut of doing it the same way year after year.

And when the complaints come, they come to me. And I can get so weary, so tired of the regularity of complaining. The topics in a local church are endless: money shortages, lack of volunteers, the old not being cared for, and the new not being welcomed. There are times when…it would be nice to just walk away.

But to where? Where would I go? There is an old saying about Noah, that if it was not for the storm on the outside, he could not bear the stink on the inside. That's the way it can be with the church and with the faith. Where else would you go?

**"HAVE I NOT CHOSEN YOU, THE TWELVE?**
**YET ONE OF YOU IS A DEVIL?"**

*JOHN 6:70*

We all dislike Judas. Judas has become a universal symbol for betrayal and disloyalty. I have yet to meet a family who decided to name their young son "Judas." Artists portray Judas on the edge of the crowd of disciples, almost always with a scowl or sneer. Yet, Jesus *chose* Judas. Jesus loved Judas. Jesus used Judas as one of his disciples. Jesus sent out Judas with the seventy.

Did Jesus make a mistake? Should he have done a better job of screening disciple candidates? Was Judas a failure on Jesus' leadership and discernment? What was the call to discipleship of Judas like anyway? How would you imagine life began as a disciple for Judas?

"**HAS NOT MOSES GIVEN YOU THE LAW? YET NOT ONE OF YOU KEEPS THE LAW. WHY ARE YOU TRYING TO KILL ME?**"
*JOHN 7:19*

I had a friend who was a strident political activist for one party. Every conversation morphed into a harangue on the idiocy of those with whom he disagreed. One day, for fun, I proposed the following scenario: his candidate was found to be both an adulterer and thief, while the opposing candidate turned out to be a committed believer and decorated patriot. Would he consider voting for the other person? "Absolutely not!" he said without batting an eye. He was against the other party no matter what.

That's how the Jewish leaders felt about Jesus. No matter what he taught, they were against him. They were not only against him; they were out to destroy him. It was about attack advantage, not truth. Where have you slipped into deep personal animosity and forgotten truth? Which adversary do you need to pray for today?

### "WHY ARE YOU ANGRY WITH ME FOR HEALING A MAN'S WHOLE BODY ON THE SABBATH?"

*JOHN 7:23*

How do you honor the Sabbath? What are your ways of keeping the Sabbath holy? I grew up in a believing family that had Sabbath-keeping traditions. There were a list of things we could not do: wash the car, go to movies, mow the lawn, go shopping, or participate in sporting practices. We could play, relax, watch TV, be with friends, and travel. But anything smacking of "work" was frowned upon. I think it was a good system overall to keep the Sabbath different from the other workdays of the week.

In Jesus' day the rules and regulations for Jews were really strict (as it is for orthodox Jews today). Anything that could be considered work or could be postponed for another day should be avoided. Healing non-life-threatening diseases was one of the prohibited activities. Yet Jesus, time and again, healed people of long-term, chronic conditions. You guessed it: the religious leaders got angry because he broke with tradition. But Jesus wanted to restructure the Sabbath into a day for glorifying God by doing good things for his creation, including healing others. It was fine if others disagreed, but why get angry? What was really behind all that anger towards Jesus—then and now?

## "WOMAN, WHERE ARE THEY?

## HAS NO ONE CONDEMNED YOU?"

### *JOHN 8:10*

The woman should be dead by now. She was caught in the very act of adultery. The punishment was death by stoning. It's interesting that no mention was made of the man who was the other party! This was the story where Jesus told them to go ahead and kill her if they were without sin themselves. And the murderous mob disappeared. When Jesus asked the woman where the crowd was, I wonder if she spent the whole time looking down at the ground, maybe with her eyes closed in terror. Did she notice the change from screaming denunciations to deathly silence?

The mob was no longer there; neither were the loud screams of condemnation. Who was accusing her now? It wasn't Jesus. Who could accuse her but herself? What is the connection between self-accusation and confession? What does Jesus do with that?

## "WHY IS MY LANGUAGE NOT CLEAR TO YOU?"

### JOHN 8:43

You've heard the joke. How can you tell if a lawyer is lying? (The answer: his or her lips are moving.) The harsh joke implies that all lawyers are liars all the time. If that is the truth, what happens to the honest lawyer? The honest lawyer faces a lifetime of assuming others always distrust whatever he or she says. That would be a hard life. In our harsh culture, there are a number of professions that are consistently the butt of jokes and the focus of anger: politicians, police, military, lawyers, religious professionals, and others. These are people who others simply do not want to hear and believe.

Why was it that even when he explained himself clearly, the religious leaders in Jesus' day did not believe him? Was there anything he could say to help them understand? Were they at all teachable? Are you?

> "CAN ANY OF YOU PROVE ME GUILTY OF SIN? IF I AM
> TELLING THE TRUTH, WHY DON'T YOU BELIEVE ME?"
> *JOHN 8:46*

*Why don't you believe* is the part of the question that rattles around in my brain. After being a pastor in churches for many years, I wonder why some people who hang around the margins just won't believe. I've visited with them, given them books, had them hear the testimonies of others, but they steadfastly refuse to believe. I don't get it.

What is the real hindrance to belief? A prior hurt and wound? Fear? Pride? Anger? What stops belief? Why don't I believe in some of the promises God makes? What about you? What keeps you from fully believing?

## "DO YOU BELIEVE IN THE SON OF MAN?"

### JOHN 9:35

This is the great story of the man born with blindness, whom Jesus heals. He gets into all sorts of trouble. The authorities grill him. His family backs away from him. The authorities kick him out of the Temple (excommunicating him!). In spite of all that, he was now seeing—though before he was blind. So Jesus came to him after all the dust settled and asked him the question above. Because he did not see the man who healed him, he asked who the Son of Man was. Jesus told him that he was the Son of Man. And the man believed. He now had a name and face for the person who made him whole.

What does it mean for you to say, "I believe"?

**"I HAVE SHOWN YOU MANY GOOD WORKS FOR THE FATHER. FOR WHICH OF THESE DO YOU STONE ME?"**

*JOHN 10:32*

"No good deed goes unpunished," the saying goes. Underneath that saying is the cynicism that an evil world punishes good actions. Jesus asked the attacking crowd to be specific. Which good works of his were most deserving of death? Which miracle warrants capital punishment? Which healing act was traitorous?

In many parts of the world, teaching young girls to read can be rewarded with an assassin's bullet. Bringing food and water to refugees can bring in the rebel thugs with guns and fire. Helping to free girls from sex trafficking can create violent backlashes. What good works around your world today are responded to with hate?

**"Is it not written in your Law, 'I have said you are 'gods.' If he called them 'gods' to whom the word of God came—and Scripture cannot be broken—what about the one whom the Father set apart as his very own and sent him into the world? Why then do you accuse me of blasphemy because I said, 'I am God's Son?'"**

*John 10:34-36*

An intelligent European woman and I were having a great conversation after dinner. She was not a church-going believer, but she was intrigued that I could be relatively rational and still be a Christian pastor. The crux of her complaint was this: "I just have such a hard time with you pushing One Truth. Every religion is true in its own way. Why are you so exclusive and judgmental?"

She was right. The truth which Christianity proclaims is exclusive: Jesus is the way, truth, and light. Jesus is the image of the invisible God. Jesus is the only Son of God. There are no others. In a pluralistic society that champions tolerance, how could proclaiming Jesus as the Son of God cause problems for you?

### "ARE THERE NOT TWELVE HOURS OF DAYLIGHT?"

*JOHN 11:9*

In the early parts of the book of John, Jesus has already intensely scrapped with Jewish religious leaders who vowed to kill him. He left Jerusalem for Bethany and to see his close friends Martha, Mary, and Lazarus. And now he signaled that he was heading back into Jerusalem. Those around him pleaded with him to delay the trip, if not cancel it. It was too dangerous. It was suicidal.

But Jesus' question was about timing and daylight. He knew he had limited time to act. His acts would be the actions of light and hope and love. Where do you sense the spiritual clock ticking in your life? Where is it time to act in the twelve hours of day?

### "WHERE HAVE YOU LAID HIM?"

### JOHN 11:34

If Jesus had a best friend, it would be Lazarus. He was not one of the twelve disciples, but a day-off buddy Jesus could hang out with. Lazarus' two sisters fussed over Jesus, but Jesus relaxed with Lazarus. When Lazarus suddenly got sick and died before Jesus turned up at Bethany, the sisters were grief-stricken and angry that Jesus did not come sooner. It was awkward. So he asked them where the body of his friend had been laid.

On the surface, this seems to be a functional question. But behind it is the question: where have you buried your dreams and hopes? Where have you laid your friendships and loves? Maybe it's a question to mature people who have had their dreams and relationships crushed and broken, and have given up dreaming and hoping. Where are they laid?

**"Did I not tell you that if you believe, you will see the glory of God?"**

*John 11:40*

Religion seems safe and reality is so, so dangerous. Religion can spout antiseptic phrases and nice platitudes, but real life is raw and unforgiving. Jesus wanted the stone that sealed the tomb rolled back into place. Martha objected, knowing the reality of decomposition and death. It would be awful! Don't do that!

Jesus refused to stay in the safe zone of future promises of eternity way off in the distance. He planned to demonstrate God's glory here and now—in a tomb with a corpse. That's glory! Where are the corpses around you, where you long to see glory? What's sealed up in your life that Jesus wants to roll away and enter into? Are you ready to see glory?

## "Do you understand what I have done for you?"

### *John 13:12*

Jesus just finished embarrassing his disciples. During a meal together, he interrupted it by taking a bowl of water and a towel and washing each one of his disciples' feet. Have you ever had someone wash your feet? I have. I didn't like it. I felt so vulnerable and weird having someone touch my feet and toes, rubbing and washing them, then toweling them dry. I wash my own feet, thank you very much! I'm into self-service in almost every area of my life.

My spiritual life also looks a lot like self-service. I practice my devotional routine. I offer up my prayers; I give my offerings. I do my works of compassion, mercy, and justice. I work pretty hard for Jesus. But do I understand what he has done—and is doing—for me? How about you?

### "WILL YOU REALLY LAY DOWN YOUR LIFE FOR ME?"
#### *JOHN 13:38*

Talk is cheap. We say stuff all the time that we don't really plan to do, but is polite to say, like *I'll be praying for you,* or *call me any time* or *we should get together sometime soon.* Our culture is filled with throwaway phrases and words nobody expects anyone to mean.

Where does your spiritual life allow throwaway phrases? Where have you allowed words to cross your lips that you don't really plan to follow up on? If you are drawing a blank or feeling defensive, take a look at the hymns and songs you sing this coming Sunday. Read the words carefully and ask, "Do I really mean that?"

I think Peter wanted to be brave and faithful to Jesus, but he did not have a clue about what that really meant. Jesus has never trafficked in throwaway phrases. Where might he be asking you "Will you really...?"

**"MY FATHER'S HOUSE HAS PLENTY OF ROOM; IF THAT WERE NOT SO, WOULD I HAVE TOLD YOU THAT I AM GOING THERE TO PREPARE A PLACE FOR YOU?"**

*JOHN 14:2*

Solipicism is a great word. It describes a developmental state of children, where what they see in front of them is an extension of themselves. They are what they see. When they see Mommy, they are happy. When they don't see Mommy, they are afraid and cry. Maturity happens when children can trust that Mommy is there, even when they can't see her.

Jesus had just finished telling his disciples a hard truth; he was going away—both for a while and for their good. They did not like the thought of not seeing and being with Jesus. His presence was the calm center for every storm. His words always brought comfort, insight, and healing. How could his absence be a good thing?

All of us reading this never experienced Jesus' physical and bodily presence. We have only known his absence from us in the body. The question is: do we believe what he promised his disciples? Do we believe he is actively preparing a place for us beyond this place in which we live now? What does it mean to your heart that Jesus is preparing another place for you?

"DON'T YOU KNOW ME PHILIP, EVEN AFTER I HAVE BEEN
AMONG YOU? ANYONE WHO HAS SEEN ME HAS SEEN THE
FATHER. HOW CAN YOU SAY 'SHOW US THE FATHER?'"

*JOHN 14:9*

When John D. Rockefeller was asked to define how much was meant by real wealth, he was reported to have replied "Just a little bit more." That is true for most of us. We cringe when we see children surrounded by Christmas gifts asking, "Are there any more?" Some of us live life with a continual hunger for just a little bit more of everything. We are constantly restless and discontent with what we have and are always on the lookout for the next thing.

Is Jesus enough for us? Are the words, work, and person of Jesus enough to satisfy our spiritual hunger? Jesus told Philip that he was all Philip needed to fully know and experience God. Jesus is sufficient. We don't need any *more*.

## "DON'T YOU BELIEVE THAT I AM IN THE FATHER, AND THE FATHER IS IN ME?"

### *JOHN 14:10*

Most religious communities really do not like mysteries. We like to explain away and define mysteries into categories that make us comfortable. Evangelicals like to domesticate Jesus and God into beneficent best friends. Liberals like to reduce Jesus into philosophical and ethical mandates that are purely intellectual. Roman Catholics like to relocate Jesus into the magisterium of the church hierarchy.

This question of Jesus is the center of the mystery of faith; Jesus and God are one. God is incarnate in Jesus, and Jesus reflects God perfectly. Do you believe that?

"**ARE YOU ASKING ONE ANOTHER WHAT I MEANT WHEN I SAID,**
'**IN A LITTLE WHILE YOU WILL SEE ME NO MORE, AND THEN**
**AFTER A LITTLE WHILE YOU WILL SEE ME?**'"

*JOHN 16:19*

*In a while* was a phrase that drove me crazy as a child. When I was anxious about when something in our family was going to happen, my father would say to me, "Just be patient. It will happen *in a while*." That was not good enough; I wanted to know *when*. Many of us live our lives in a hurry and exhausted, and we're continually running out of time.

Pause for a moment today. Imagine your spiritual life as a clock face with twelve hours on it. What time is it in your spiritual life? How does time describe who you are in Christ? What did you wait for that you have now experienced? What are you experiencing right now in your walk with Christ? What are you still waiting for?

### "DO YOU NOW BELIEVE?"

*JOHN 16:31*

How many more sermons do I need to preach? How many more Sunday School classes need to be taught? How many more Bible studies do you need to be attend? How many more devotional books do you need to read? How much more do you need in your life to experience mature belief?

I think we pastors are guilty of cultivating perpetual spiritual adolescence among our congregations, in order keep people coming back for more (of our preaching and teaching and giving). Jesus' question is so ultimate: *do you now believe?* Are you ready to step up into spiritual adulthood and maturity? What more do you need?

## "WHO IS IT YOU WANT?"
### JOHN 18:4, 7

Jesus asked this question twice. He went to the angry mob at night in the garden and asked them the question above. The heart of the question for me is centered on the word *want*. Who does the crowd *want?* Who does Judas *want?* Who do the onlookers *want?* Who do the disciples *want?* Who do you *want?*

**"PUT YOUR SWORD AWAY! SHALL I NOT DRINK THE CUP THE FATHER HAS GIVEN ME?"**

*JOHN 18:11*

In most conflict situations, the side or person with the most power wins. Who has the power varies by the context. In some settings, power is defined by the ones with the most money or votes. In other settings, however, power falls to those with the most force or weaponry. Jesus redirects the question of power away from swords to God's will (the cup). The power belongs to God, who gave Jesus the privilege, task, and burden of laying down his life for us. There was no real power in the swords of the mob or of the disciples. Where do you sense the driving power in your life? Where is the urgency of God's will for you?

**"I SAID NOTHING IN SECRET.**

**WHY QUESTION ME?"**

*JOHN 18:21*

Clubs traffic in secrets. Every secret society or exclusive club holds some secret information known only to insiders. It's what makes belonging to a fraternal society so appealing; *I know the secret, and you don't! I'm on the inside, and you're not!*

There are no secrets with Jesus. What Jesus taught and accomplished, he did in the open for all to see. There are no secret inner truths. Yes, there are mysteries, but they are mysteries for all of us. Where have you been trapped by secrets or held hostage by secrets? How can Jesus set you free?

**"BUT IF I SPOKE THE TRUTH,**

**WHY DID YOU STRIKE ME?"**

*JOHN 18:23*

Did the mob that arrested Jesus and gathered him for a *trial* really want to know the truths of the case, or were they just looking to achieve a predetermined outcome? Was there any genuine inquiry, or was it all a sham? Did they ask real questions to Jesus, or were they traps? Here we see one of the most profound differences between Jesus and the religious leaders of his day. He asked real questions and delivered genuine answers. And for that he was flogged and eventually crucified!

How badly do you want truth today, or how much do you want validation of your already-formed opinions? How willing are you to allow Jesus' truth to change your mind?

**"IS THIS YOUR OWN IDEA, OR DID
OTHERS TALK TO YOU ABOUT ME?"**

*JOHN 18:34*

Where do you get your ideas? Jesus was asking that question to the most politically powerful man in his day—Pontius Pilate. Pilate asked Jesus if he was "the king of the Jews." That was the rumor and accusation being circulated to demand Jesus' execution, that he was a rival king to Herod.

"Where did that idea come from?" Jesus asked Pilate. "Who informs your opinions?" Jesus asks us. Who else shapes your opinions today? What newscaster or writer seeds your mind with ideas? Whose voice do you grant access to your opinion making? Where did you get your ideas about church, discipleship, faithfulness, and serving?

## "WOMAN, WHY ARE YOU CRYING?
## WHO IS IT YOU ARE LOOKING FOR?"
### *JOHN 20:15*

The question *why* is directly related to the question *who*. Mary had seen too much. She saw Jesus arrested. She saw Jesus crucified. She saw Jesus' dead body. She saw Jesus wrapped and lying in the tomb. She saw her world die as Jesus died. She was looking for the last scrap of her life—the dead body of Jesus to finish preparing for burial—and now it too was gone, taken, stolen. It was too much; it was raw grief and exhaustion. Of course she wept. Insult was added to injury.

Some of us have a long list of our losses, disappointments, failures, and betrayals. As we age, pessimism grows in place of hope. We no longer trust the promises of the best leaders and pastors. We have seen them come and go before. We are just looking for the dead bodies and shattered dreams to clean up and put away. What if Jesus approached you today and asked you the same question: *who are you looking for?* What would be your answer?

## "FRIENDS, HAVEN'T YOU ANY FISH?"

### JOHN 21:5

I have a fallback plan. If I could not be a pastor, there are a number of other jobs I would consider trying to do. I think I could be of help at a funeral home. I might be a good waiter. I'd like to try driving a bus. Those are things I could do, I think.

The disciples had a fallback plan as well: fishing. It was the profession they did before following Jesus. Now that he was dead, it was what they could do to support themselves, but they weren't always successful. On this day, they struck out. There were no fish to be caught after being out on the water all night.

Was Jesus' question to them a jab at their incompetence? Or was Jesus reminding them that he was in charge, even of their fallback plans? Didn't he know where the fish were? They still needed to follow him to find any semblance of success and fulfillment. What simple word of advice or recommendation is Jesus giving you today about your normal routine? On which side of the boat is he telling you to cast your nets?

## "SIMON, SON OF JOHN,

### DO YOU LOVE ME MORE THAN THESE?"

*JOHN 21:15-17*

I once had a falling out with a guy. His wife was on staff, and she left the church. He blamed me for poor leadership (partly right) and publicly exploded on me after worship, in the narthex, with crowds around him. It unraveled me. Church leaders stepped in and worked through reconciliation following Matthew 18 to no avail. He would not talk with me or seek reconciliation. He and his wife left the church very angry.

I bumped into him several times in the following years, in airports and stores. His response was to physically turn and walk away. It was maddening. There was nothing I could do. Years later, after I left the church to serve another one, I happened to be back in town for a family celebration. All of a sudden I saw him, and he saw me. Instead of walking away, he walked toward me, with his arms out. We hugged and I wept. "I'm sorry," was all either of us said. We could not stop hugging each other. Reconciliation needed face-to-face contact to be realized.

Jesus approached Simon Peter three times after breakfast on the shore. Three times he asked him the same question: "Do you love me?" Three times Simon said, "Yes." Three times Simon denied knowing Jesus. It required face-to-face contact to be reconciled to Jesus. Who are those ones with whom you long to be reconciled today? Bring their names and faces before God right now in prayer.

## "IF I WANT HIM TO REMAIN ALIVE UNTIL I RETURN, WHAT IS THAT TO YOU?"

*JOHN 21:22, 23*

I love the disciples because they can be so petty—just like me. They have gone through everything: three years of being in the daily presence of Jesus, witnessing Jesus' death and resurrection, and hearing Jesus teach about the future and their roles. This is high-octane life!

Yet when Peter saw the disciple whom Jesus loved (most likely John) following closely, he got jealous and asked *what about him?* It's the petty question of people who still don't want others to get more than they have. It's the cry children make when they say *that's not fair!*

Why do we worry about what God's plans are for others? Why do we worry about others doing better than we are doing? Why are my eyes set on others and not on God? *What is that to me and to you?*

# 3<sup>RD</sup> ANGEL QUESTION

**"DO YOU KNOW WHY I HAVE COME TO YOU?"**

*DAN. 10:20*

Daniel was a faithful servant of God, who lived in an overtly pagan world. He was continually challenged to follow God's ways even against the patterns and norms of his community. It was risky and it was costly. The lion's den incident happened back in chapter 6.

God came to him in a vision with angels with the question above. *Do you know why* is a great question for all of us. Why has God allowed you to be born in the nation in which you live? Why has God gifted you with the talents and abilities you have? Why has God given you the faith community that surrounds you? Do you have a deep sense of purpose? Why might God be using you now?

Made in the USA
Lexington, KY
12 September 2017